The Photographer's

BUSINESS
and
LEGAL

Handbook

By Leonard D. DuBoff
Attorney

The Photographer's Business and Legal Handbook

ISBN: 0-929667-02-6
Library of Congress Catalog Card Number: 89-080893

Published by
  Images Press
  22 East 17th Street
  New York, N.Y. 10003

Book Design and Typesetting by *FAST TYPE, Inc.*
Manufactured in the United States of America
10 9 8 7 6 5 4 3 2 1

DEDICATION

To Cumi Elena Rhodes Crawford for her love
and her daughter.

CONTENTS

FOREWORD

If you're a professional photographer you must own this book. It's as basic and valuable a tool as your light meter.

Leonard D. DuBoff's *The Photographer's Business and Legal Handbook* will help you avoid some legal pitfalls, answer many legal questions about our business, and intelligently inform you how to deal with your own legal counsel (something hard to avoid these days!).

Professor DuBoff says, "Most legal problems cost more to solve or defend than it would have cost to prevent their occurrence in the first place."

That's the bottom line. By reading this thoughtful and informative work you can practice what DuBoff preaches.

David Hume Kennerly

PREFACE

I have been asked by the many photographers I represent to provide them with the name of a text which would help them understand the myriad of legal problems that are prevalent in the world of photography. Unfortunately, I have been unable to locate such a book. I therefore decided to undertake the task of creating one which would enable the professional photographer to learn about the legal problems which can and do arise in this profession. It is my hope that this book will serve this purpose.

This text is not intended to be a substitute for a lawyer, rather, it is designed to educate professional photographers about potential legal pitfalls and traps so that they can be avoided. It is also designed to assist the professional photographer with legal vocabulary and concepts so that discussions with an attorney will be more efficient. Since a lawyer's time costs money, it was my goal to provide a practical, readable and understandable volume for you, the professional photographer, so that you can either avoid legal entanglements or when necessary, seek professional assistance before a problem becomes irreparable. It is my sincere hope that this book will fulfill my expectations and your needs.

ACKNOWLEDGMENTS

I could not have completed the arduous, yet pleasurable, task of amassing the numerous cases and materials necessary to create this volume without the help of many friends, colleagues and former students. I am extremely indebted to them for their encouragement, support and assistance. In particular, I would like to thank my research assistant, Ms. Lila Lee, J.D. 1987, for her skill and diligence. I would also like to thank Ms. Georgene Inaba, J.D. 1985; Greta Gibbs, J.D. 1984; Alice Bennison, J.D. 1987; Mary Stasack, J.D. 1980; and Nancy Walseth, J.D. 1978; for help with the mechanics of preparing a manuscript for publication.

When I first met the Pulitzer Prize winning photographer, David Hume Kennerly, in Asia many years ago, I never realized that our paths would once again cross. I was therefore extremely honored when he consented to write the Introduction to this text.

I would also like to thank photographers Steve Meltzer and Jennifer Werner for reading a draft of the manuscript and for providing me with many useful and practical comments.

I once again would like to thank Lenair Mulford for her extreme patience and skill in converting a collection of notes, scraps, interlineations and cross-outs into a publishable manuscript. Lenair's lightening fingers and pinpoint accuracy have once again blossomed in this volume.

My children, Colleen Rose DuBoff, Robert Courtney DuBoff, and Sabrina Ashley DuBoff were deprived of their father's company during the period while this manuscript was created. I thank them for their understanding and hope that this work is meritorious enough to reward the sacrifice.

Finally, and most important, I would like to acknowledge the valuable contribution of my partner in law and in life, Mary Ann Crawford DuBoff. She has once again inspired and assisted me with the project which has emerged as *The Photographer's Business and Legal Handbook*. This book could not have been written without her help.

Leonard DuBoff, Portland, Oregon 1989

The Photographer's

BUSINESS
and
LEGAL

Handbook

By Leonard D. DuBoff
Attorney

Chapter 1

COPYRIGHT LAW

The professional photographer is hardly likely to have a staff lawyer. So, in addition to becoming skilled at your work and getting word out to the rest of the world, you need to have an awareness of what potential legal problems may be lurking in your business dealings. Once you are armed with the knowledge of what to look for, you can usually avoid potentially serious headaches.

Copyright protection is a good topic for starting this book. It is a subject about which most photographers have many questions, and it is also a legal matter that—barring infringement problems—you can usually handle yourself.

Copyright law in the United States has its foundations in the Constitution, which provides in Article I, section 8 that Congress shall have the power "to promote the progress of science and the useful arts, by securing for limited time to authors and inventors the exclusive right to their respective writings and discoveries." The first Congress exercised this power and enacted a copyright law, which has been periodically revised by later Congresses.

The Copyright Act expressly provides for the registration of photographs. Furthermore, photography has been adjudicated by the courts as being eligible for copyright protection because photography is a form of creative expression and each photograph involves artistic choices. According to the United States Supreme Court, a photograph "must be deemed a work of art and its maker an author, inventor or designer of it, within the meaning and protection of the copyright statute."

The Copyright Act of 1909 remained in effect for more than half a century despite periodic complaints that it no longer reflected contemporary technology. At the time the 1909 Act was passed, the printing press was still the primary means of disseminating information. But new technology such as improved printing processes, radio, television, videotape, computer software, and microfilm created the need for a revision that would provide specific statutory copyright protection for newer information systems.

The 1909 Act was substantially revised in 1976. The Copyright Revision Act of 1976 became effective on January 1, 1978, and covers works created or published on or after that date. The creation of copyright in all works published prior to January 1, 1978 is governed by the 1909 Act. Rights other than creation, such as duration of copyright, infringement penalties, and infringement remedies are governed by the new law. It is important to be aware of the basic differences in the two laws, and of which law applies to a given work.

The 1976 Act was a product of compromise. Many of the clauses of the Act were drafted to appease competing special-interest groups. As a result, much of the language is ambiguous. In time these ambiguities will be clarified by the courts, but for now parts of modern copyright law resemble a guessing game. In 1988 Congress once again amended the statute so that the United States could become a party to the Berne Convention, a major copyright treaty. For the first time in the history of American copyright law, a copyright notice will no longer be required; although, as discussed later, it should be used wherever possible.

Clearly, you as a photographer need to know what protection you have under the present law, and the information in this chapter should be pertinent to you. Be aware, though, that if you sell photographs to advertisers or publishers, they may take care of the details of copyright notice, deposit, and registration, so you may not need to concern yourself about dealing with the Copyright Office. Check your contract, of course, to make sure that the copyright is to be in your name.

Federal Preemption of State Copyright Law

One of the problems with the 1909 Act was that it was not the exclusive source of copyright law. Copyright protection or its equivalent was also provided by common law (that body of law developed by the courts independent of statutes) and various state laws. This caused considerable confusion since securing copyright protection or avoiding copyright infringement required careful examination of a variety of different laws.

The 1976 Act largely resolved this problem by pre-empting and nullifying all other copyright law — in other words, it is now the only legislation generally governing copyright protection. The Act does not, however, pre-empt the common law or the statutes of any state for copyright claims arising prior to January 1, 1978.

What Is Copyright?

A copyright is actually a collection of five exclusive rights. First is the right to reproduce a work by any means. The scope of this right can be hard to define, especially when it involves photocopying, microform, videotape, and the like. Under the Copyright Act of 1976, someone may reproduce protected works only if such reproduction involves either a fair or an exempted use as defined by the Act, which I will be explaining later in this chapter.

Second is the right to prepare derivative works based on the copyrighted work. *A derivative work* is one that transforms or adapts the subject matter of one or more preexisting works. Derivative works of a photograph might include use in a composite, as well as adaptations into another medium such as television, film, or a painting.

Third is the right to distribute copies to the public for sale or lease. However, once a photographer sells a print, the right to control the further use of that very print is, usually, ended. This should be distinguished from the copyright in the print which can only be conveyed in a signed writing. When you sell the print alone, you are selling the physical piece, not the right to reproduce it. This rule, known as the *first-sale doctrine*, does not apply if the work is merely in the possession of someone else temporarily by virtue of bailment,* rental, lease, or loan. In these instances the copyright owner retains the right to control the further sale or other disposition of the work. Moreover, the first-sale doctrine does not apply if the copyright owner has a contract with the purchaser restricting the purchaser's freedom to use the work. In such a case, if the purchaser exceeds the restrictions, there may be liability. In this situation the copyright owner's remedy will be governed by con-

tract law rather than copyright law.

You should distinguish between a sale of a print and a sale of the copyright in that print. If nothing is said about the copyright when the print is sold, you will retain the copyright. Since purchasers may not be aware of this, you may wish to call it to their attention either in the sales memorandum or on the back of the photo. If a license to reprint is granted, it should be in writing and you should be very specific about its scope. For example, may a person who has purchased the right to use a photograph in a newspaper ad also use it in a magazine? Generally, the answer is no but you should be clear in defining the boundaries of permissible uses.

Fourth is the right to perform the work publicly — for example, in the case of an audio/visual work, to broadcast a film on television, or show it in a theater.

Fifth is the right to display the work publicly. Once the copyright owner has sold a copy of the photograph, however, the owner of the copy has the right to display that copy but generally does not have permission to reproduce it.

Who Owns the Copyright?

The general rule regarding ownership of copyright is that the *photographer* — the creator — of a print is the owner of the copyright in it. Under the old law, which still applies to photographs taken before January 1, 1978, when a photograph was sold, ownership of a common-law copyright was presumed to pass to the purchaser of that photograph unless the photographer explicitly provided otherwise in a written agreement. In other words, there was a presumption in the law that a sale included not only the photograph itself, but all rights in that work. However, by specifically granting a customer only the nonexclusive use rights of a copy of the photograph (for instance, to use a photograph in an advertisement), the photographer would have retained the copyright, since such permission is not equivalent to assignment of the copyright.

Before the Copyright Act of 1976, the employer, subject, boss, client or customer owned the negative, all prints and all use rights in a photograph unless the parties contractually agreed otherwise. Thus, the customer owned the negative and the right to sell or license the use of the negative, or the right to use it himself commercially or in advertising.

In *White Studio, Inc. v. Dreyfoos*, the court held that

---

*Bailment is the legal temporary possession of someone else's property; parking a car in a paid parking lot establishes a bailment; so does leaving a film with a developer.

the agreement between a photographer and customer constitutes a contract pursuant to which photographers are employees of their customers. Under this view, both conception and production of the photograph were work done for the customer and thus the customer was the exclusive owner of all proprietary rights. Later, in 1946, a court ruled that custom and usage could not be set up to oppose or to modify the general rule of law that all proprietary rights to photographs vest in the customer.

The case of *Colten v. Jacques Marthais, Inc.* specifically extended to photography the rule that all rights in a picture belonged to the customer. The court held that the relationship between a commercial photographer and an advertising agency was no different from that between a portrait photographer and a customer.

Although a photographer was allowed to retain possession of the negative, the photographer did not have the right to print additional copies from it. This policy was based on either the theory of an implied contractual restriction or on the grounds of the right of privacy.

Today, it is possible that in some circumstances a court would have found an implied contract between a commercial photographer and a publishing company or advertising agency, that the company or agency would return photographs or negatives submitted on approval that it did not intend to use. A much clearer situation would be a photographer who solicited a person to come to her studio and took photographs for the photographer's own benefit and at her own expense. Here the copyright would vest in the photographer.

The Copyright Act of 1976 reverses the presumption that the sale of a photograph carries the copyright with it. Today, unless there is a written agreement that transfers the copyright to the customer, the photographer retains the copyright.

If a photographer owns the copyright, she also automatically owns the exclusive rights. The photographers of a *joint work* are co-owners of the copyright in the work. A joint work is a work prepared by more than one person "with the intention that their contributions be merged into inseparable or interdependent parts of a unitary whole." Thus, whatever profit one creator makes from use of the work must be shared equally with the others unless they have a written agreement that states otherwise. If there is no intention to create a unitary, or indivisible, work, each creator may own the copyright to that creator's individual contribution. For example, one creator may own the rights to written material and another the rights in the illustrative photographs.

Works for Hire

Works considered to be *works for hire* are an important exception to the general rule that a photographer owns the copyright in a picture he or she has taken. If a photograph was taken by an employee on the job, the law considers the picture a work for hire, and the employer will own the copyright. However, the parties involved may avoid application of this rule if they write their contract carefully. If the employment contract itself provides, for example, that creating the copyrightable material in question is not part of the "scope of employment," the employee will likely be considered the owner of the copyright and the work for hire doctrine will not apply.

In *Peregrine v. Lauren Corp.*, the court found that a photographer was working for hire when the employing advertising agency had the right to supervise and control the photographer's work. Courts also considered the amount of an employer's artistic advice before, during and after the photographic session when determining whether a photographer was working for hire as opposed to working as an independent contractor. (An independent contractor is someone hired on a one-time or job-by-job basis, as opposed to a permanent employee.) Some courts developed a doctrine whereby an independent contractor was considered to be a "special employee" for copyright purposes when a commissioning party had the right to exercise control over the work. This resulted in the commissioning party owning the copyright rather than the independent contractor. In 1989 the United States Supreme Court in *Community for Creating Non-Violence (CCNV) v. Reid* held that unless the party creating the work is an actual employee, as that term is defined in the law, the copyright will belong to him rather than the commissioning party. The court did leave open the question of whether the work could be considered a joint work by virtue of the parties' intent. There is no question that a professional portrait photographer owns the copyright in the photographs he creates and is not considered to be creating works for hire.

If the photographer is an independent contractor, the photographs will be considered works for hire only if (1) the parties have signed a written agreement to that effect and (2) the work is specially ordered or commissioned as a contribution to a collective work, a supplementary work (one that introduces, revises, comments upon or assists a work by another), a compilation, an instructional text, answer material for a test, an atlas, motion picture, or an audio-visual work. Thus, if there is no contractual agreement to the contrary, the photographer who is an independent contractor will own the copyright on these works.

Transferring or Licensing the Copyright

A copyright owner may sell the entire copyright or any part of it, or may license any right within it. To accomplish this there must be a written document that describes the rights conveyed. The document should be signed by the copyright owner or the owner's duly authorized agent. A license authorizing a particular use of a work can be granted orally, but it will be revocable at the will of the copyright owner. In addition to reducing a license to writing, you should be clear on the scope of rights granted. Is the purchaser of a license permitted only a one-time use or multiple uses? By specifying the exact uses conveyed, you may avoid becoming involved in a battle over rights.

It is not uncommon for a photographer to become the assignee or licensee of another person's copyright. This could happen, say, when a photographer wishes to incorporate another person's illustrations, photographs, recordings, writings, or other work into the photographer's work; in this case the photographer will often enter into a licensing agreement or assignment of ownership with the other person. Such an agreement is necessary to authorize use of the copyrighted work.

Both an assignment of ownership and a licensing agreement can, and should, be recorded with the Copyright Office. When the transaction is recorded, the rights of the assignee or licensee are protected by recording a deed — in much the same way as the rights of an owner of real estate are protected. In a case of conflicting transfers of rights, if both transactions are recorded within one month of the execution, the person whose transaction was completed first will prevail. If the transactions are not recorded within a month, the one who records first will prevail. A non-exclusive license will prevail over any unrecorded transfer of ownership. Finally, before a transferee (either an assignee or licensee) can sue a third party for infringement, the document of transfer must be recorded. The cost to record a transfer is only ten dollars and is tax-deductible if it is a business expense. Considering the potential consequences of not re-cording a transfer of rights, the assignee or licensee is well advised to record.

One section of the 1976 Copyright Act pertains to the involuntary transfer of a copyright. This section, which states that such a transfer will be held invalid, was included primarily because of problems arising from U.S. recognition of foreign copyrights. For example, if a country did not want a photographer's controversial work to be published, it could claim to be the copyright owner and thereby refuse to license foreign publication. Under the 1976 Act, the foreign government must produce a signed record of the transfer before its ownership will be recognized. Another situation covered in this section of the Act deals with a transfer that at first glance might appear to be involuntary but is not. This is the case where the courts transfer a copyright in a bankruptcy proceeding or in the foreclosure of a mortgage secured by the copyright. Such a transfer is considered voluntary rather than involuntary because the copyright owner freely chose to declare bankruptcy or to mortgage the copyright, even though the owner may not have chosen the consequences.

Termination of Copyright Transfers and Licenses

It has not been unusual for a photographer confronted with an unequal bargaining position vis-a-vis an ad agency to transfer all rights in the copyright to the agency for a pittance, only to see the work become valuable at a later date. The 1976 Copyright Act, in response to this injustice, provides that after a certain period has lapsed, the photographer or certain other parties may terminate the transfer of the copyright and reclaim the rights. Thus, the new Act grants the photographer a second chance to exploit a work after the original transfer of copyright. This right to terminate a transfer is called a *termination interest*.

In most cases, the termination interest will belong to the photographer. But if the photographer is no longer alive and is survived by a spouse but no children, the surviving spouse owns the termination interest. If the deceased photographer is not survived by a spouse, ownership of the interest belongs to any surviving children in equal shares. If the decedent is survived by both spouse and children, the interest is divided so that the spouse receives 50 percent and the children receive the remaining 50 percent in equal proportions.

Where the termination interest is owned by more than one party, be they other photographers or a photographer's survivors, a majority of the owners must agree to terminate the transfer. Under the new Act, the general rule is that termination may be effected at any time within a five-year period beginning at the end of the thirty-fifth year from the date on which the rights were transferred. If, however, the transfer included the right of publication, termination may go into effect at any time within a five-year period beginning at the end of thirty-five years from the date of publication, or forty years from the date of transfer, whichever is shorter.

The party wishing to terminate the transferred interest must serve an advance written notice on the transferee. This notice must state the intended termination date and must be served not less than two and no more than ten years prior to the stated termination date. A copy of the notice must be recorded in the Copyright Office before the effective date of termination.

What Can Be Copyrighted?

The Constitution permits Congress to provide protection for a limited time to *authors* for their *writings*. An author, from the point of view of copyright law, may be the creator—be it a photographer, sculptor, writer, or the employer in a work-for-hire situation; there have been debates over what constitutes a writing, but it is now clear that this term includes photographs. Congress avoided use of the word *writings* in describing the scope of copyright protection. Instead it grants copyright protection to "original works of authorship fixed in any tangible medium of expression." Legislative comments on this section of the Act suggest that Congress chose to use this wording rather than *writings* in order to have more leeway to legislate in the copyright field.

The 1976 Act expressly exempts from copyright protection "any idea, procedure, process, system, method of operation, concept, principle, or discovery." In short, a copyright extends only to the *expression* of creations of the mind, not to the ideas themselves. Frequently there is no clear line of division between an idea and its expression, a problem which will be considered in greater detail in the "Infringement and Remedies" section of this chapter. For now, it is sufficient to note that a pure idea, such as a plan to photograph something in a certain manner, cannot be copyrighted no matter how original or creative it is.

The law and the courts generally avoid using copyright law to arbitrate the public's taste. Thus, a work is not denied a copyright even if it makes no pretense to aesthetic or academic merit. The only requirements are that a work be original and show some creativity. Originality—as distinguished from uniqueness—requires that a photograph be taken independently, but does not require that it be the only one of its kind. In other words, a photograph of underwater algae in the Antarctic is copyrightable for its creative aspects; the unusual, hard-to-shoot subject matter is irrelevant.

In the past, the Copyright Office occasionally denied protection to works considered immoral or obscene, even though it had no express authority for doing so. Today this practice has changed. The Copyright Office will not attempt to decide whether a work is obscene or not, and copyright registration will not be refused because of the questionable character of any work.

Not everything in a copyrighted work is protected. Photographers should be aware that, for example, the title of a photograph cannot be copyrighted. Writers have the problem of whether a fictional character can be protected by copyright.

Under the 1909 Act, most photographs that qualified for copyright had to be published with the proper notice attached in order to get statutory protection. The 1976 Act dramatically changes the law in this respect. A photographer's pictures are now automatically copyrighted once they are "fixed in a tangible medium of expression." The photographer's product is considered to have been fixed in a tangible medium of expression as soon as he clicks the shutter and an image is created on film. The photograph need not be developed to be protected. However, after the 1976 Act and prior to the 1988 amendment, a copyright could be lost if a photograph was published without the proper notice, unless the "savings clause" from Section 405 of the Act applied. (The savings clause enables a photographer to save a copyright in certain situations.) For further discussion of retrieving copyright protection after publication without notice prior to March 1, 1988. See "Deposit and Registration" later in this chapter.

Once the copyright on a work has expired, or been lost, the work enters the public domain, where it can be exploited by anyone in any manner. A photographer can, however, get a copyright on a work derived from a work in the public domain if a distinguishable variation is created. This means, for example, that Rembrandt's "Night Watch" cannot be copyrighted, but a photograph of it can. As a result, no one would be able to copy the photograph, whereas anyone can copy Rembrandt's original. The photograph is thus a copyrightable derivative work of a pre-existing work. Other examples of copyrightable derivative works would include collages, photographs of photographs, film versions, and any other work "recast, transformed, or adapted" from an original.

Compilations are also copyrightable, as long as the pre-existing materials are gathered and arranged in a new or original form. Compilations such as magazines, pamphlets or books can be copyrightable as a whole even though individual contributions or photographs are individually copyrighted.

Publication

In copyright law, the concept of publication is different from what a lay person might expect it to be. *Publication*, according to the 1976 Act, is the *distribution of copies of a work to the public* by sale or other transfer of ownership, or by rental, lease, or loan. A public performance or display of a work does not of itself constitute publication. And, under the *doctrine of limited publication*, publication will not be deemed to have occurred when a photographer displays work "to a definitely selected group and for a limited purpose, without the right of diffusion, reproduction, distribution or sale."

Under the Copyright Act of 1909, when a photographer showed copies of a picture to close friends or associates with the understanding that such copies were not to be further reproduced and distributed, the photographer had not published the pictures, nor would the distribution of pictures to agents or customers for purposes of review and criticism constitute a publication. Thus, even an exhibition in a gallery or museum where copying or photographing the work was prohibited probably would not have constituted publication. In *American Tobacco Co. v. Werkmeister*, the Supreme Court held that museum exhibition was not publication even though admission was charged and copying and photographing of the work was prohibited.

The Copyright Revision Act of 1976 makes no specific reference to this doctrine of limited publication. The statutory definition of publication does, however, require a "distribution of copies or phonorecords of a work to the public." A congressional report explains that "the public" in this context refers to people who are under no explicit or implicit restrictions with respect to disclosure of the work's contents. This appears to suggest that the current Act is continuing the doctrine of limited publication.

Duration of Copyright

The Constitution permits Congress to grant copyright protection only "for limited times." The 1909 Copyright Act granted a creator copyright protection for a twenty-eight-year period which could be renewed for only one additional twenty-eight-year period. Under the 1976 Act, copyright exists during the life of the creator plus fifty years. There are no renewals for copyrights created under the 1976 Act. However, the 1976 Act does provide renewals for copyrights which were created under the 1909 Act and were not yet in their final renewal term when the 1976 Act became effective. Thus, copyrights granted under the 1909 Act and still in their first twenty-eight-year term as of January 1, 1978, will continue for the remainder of the twenty-eight-year term and can be renewed for another forty-seven years. Copyrights granted under the 1909 Act and in their second twenty-eight-year term as of January 1, 1978, will automatically receive an extension of the number of years that would create a term of seventy-five years from the date copyright was first obtained. Applications for renewal must be made within one year before the first term ends. In all cases, copyright terms end on December 31 of the given year.

A photographer may assign the right to renew a copyright granted under the 1909 Act. In order for the renewal to be effective, the assignee must renew in the photographer's name. Since the assignee can act only in the name of the photographer, the assignment right becomes void after the photographer dies. In such cases the renewal right reverts to the photographer's legal survivors.

As previously noted, the employer who owns the copyright in a photograph taken by an employee in the scope of employment is considered the author of the work and therefore owns the renewal right. However, if the employer should assign the renewal rights and then die before the renewal, the right does not revert to the employer's heirs. Since the 1909 statute did not distinguish between works by employees and works by independent contractors in works made for hire, there is some question as to whether the renewal rights on commissioned works revert to the photographer's heirs upon the photographer's death.

If the copyrighted work is a joint work, any of the photographers involved may renew for the benefit of all. If the copyrights are owned separately, each photographer must renew individually. The copyright in a composite work, such as an illustrated book, can be renewed by the owner of the copyright even if the owner was not a writer or photographer.

For copyrights created under the 1976 Act, there is no renewal and thus no right to assign a renewal. If the work is created by one photographer, it is copyrighted for the rest of the photographer's life plus fifty years. If the work was created jointly, the copyright expires fifty years after the last photographer dies. The Copyright Office has been keeping records of famous photographers' deaths since the mid-1960s, but if the office does not have a record of a photographer's death, the photographer is assumed dead seventy-five years after the first publication date or a hundred years after creation, whichever occurs first. A composite work or a work for hire is copyrighted for seventy-five years after publication or a hundred years from creation, whichever expires first. The same applies to anonymous and pseudonymous works.

Unpublished works which were fixed in a tangible medium prior to January 1, 1978 form their own special category for purposes of determining the duration of copyright protection. Since they are unpublished, they do not come under the 1909 Act. But since they were fixed in a tangible medium prior to January 1, 1978, they do not automatically come under the 1976 Act. Prior to the 1976 Act, these types of works were covered by state law, which protected them in perpetuity. The 1976 Act extends federal protection for these works for a limited amount of time: the author's life plus fifty years. The Act also provides that the earliest date when such a copyright can expire is December 31, 2002. If the work is published before that date, the term of copyright shall not expire before December 31, 2027, a twenty-five year extension. There are many unpublished works whose creators are now dead. If photographers such as Ansel Adams or Imogen Cunningham left unpublished works which are published in the future, the statute has not deprived these works of their potential value to their owners, since protection is automatically extended until December 31, 2002. However, the statute does encourage owners of unpublished photographs to publish these works before December 31, 2002, in order to obtain the twenty-five-year extension.

Creation of Copyright

As discussed earlier, all works are now automatically protected by the federal copyright law as soon as they are fixed in a tangible medium. There are no formal requirements of registration or deposit of copies. Unpublished works can be registered with the Copyright Office, and it is necessary that registration have taken place if an infringement suit is going to be filed. A prepublication registration can be made *after* the infringement, though, as long as the registration occurs before filing suit. One of the advantages to early registration is that after five years the facts contained in the registration are presumed to be true in an infringement case. This presumption, which will carry over even after the work is published, can greatly simplify the copyright owner's preparation for trial.

Copyright Notice

Works published under the 1909 Act had to contain the proper notice in order to be copyrighted. With few exceptions, any omission, misplacement, or imperfection in the notice on any copy of a work distributed by authority of the copyright owner placed the work forever in the public domain. Thus it was important for the copyright owner, when signing a contract, to make sure that granting a license to publish be conditioned on the publisher's inclusion of the proper copyright notice. That way, if the publisher made a mistake in the notice, the publication might be deemed unauthorized but the copyright would not be affected. The publisher could be liable to the copyright owner for the loss of copyright if it did occur.

Since notice is an inflexible requirement for works published before January 1, 1978, it is important to determine when publication occurred. Although notice is no longer required under the new law, the publication date is still of some importance under the new law. For example, the duration of the copyright of a work for hire is measured from either creation or first publication.

Location of Copyright Notice

Since March 1, 1988, a copyright notice is no longer required to be affixed to a work. Nevertheless, it is a good idea to use the notice since it will make others aware of your rights. The Copyright Office had required that the copyright notice for a photograph appear either on the front or back of the image or, in the case of a transparency, on the cardboard frame. A rubber stamp can make the job easy and it may be more legible.

Wording of a Copyright Notice

Even though it is no longer necessary to place a notice on your work, it still should be used whenever possible. A copyright notice has three elements. First there must be the word *copyright*, the abbreviation Copr., or the letter c in a circle, ©. No variations are permitted. Second is the year of first publication (or, in the case of unpublished works governed by the 1909 Act, the year in which the copyright was registered). This date may be expressed in Arabic or Roman numerals or in words. Under the 1909 Act it was not clear when a derivative (or revised) work—for example, a composite of photographs in a collage—was first published. To be safe, both dates, that of the original work and that of the revision, were usually given. The 1976 Act makes it clear that the date of the first publication of the revised work is sufficient. The year of the first publication can be omitted on certain works designated in the Act, but this category is extremely narrow. Since the date is necessary for some international protection, it should always be included. The third necessary element, following the date of publication, is the name of the copyright owner. If there are several, one name is sufficient. Usually the author's full name is used, but if the author is well known by a last name, the last name can be used alone or with initials. A business that owns a copyright may use its trade name if the name is legally recognized in its state. Copyright notice for a photograph by the author of this book would either be Copr. 1989 Leonard DuBoff or © 1989 Leonard DuBoff.

Copyright notice should be used to avoid having someone copy the work in the belief it is in the public domain. Even though the 1976 Act allows the photographer to save the copyright on works published without notice and the 1988 revision does not require notice, someone who copies work believing it's in the public domain because there is no notice is considered an innocent infringer under the statute. In this situation, the photographer whose work was copied cannot recover damages; in fact, a court might allow the copier to continue using the work. The 1988 amendment also provides that if the notice is used, then there is a presumption that an infringer cannot be innocent.

If international protection is desired, the copyright owner may have to add to the copyright notice. For example, under the Buenos Aires Convention (which includes most Central and South American countries as well as the United States), the statement *all rights reserved*, in either Spanish or English, must be included in the notice. If there is any possibility that the work will be sold in Central or South America, it would be advisable to include this statement. Another agreement, the Universal Copyright Con-

vention (UCC), requires the use of the international copyright symbol, ©, accompanied by the name of the copyright owner and the year of first publication. If these requirements are met, any formalities required by the domestic law of a UCC signatory country are deemed to have been satisfied. The protection in the country where the work is sold will then be the same as whatever protection that country accords its own nationals. Most European nations have signed the UCC, as has the United States. However, UCC protection is available only for American works first published in the United States after the convention became effective, which was on September 16, 1955. Thus, works first published in the United States before that date are not entitled to UCC protection. Nevertheless, such works will have international protection under another agreement—the Berne Convention—if the works were simultaneously published in the U.S. and a Berne signatory country.

The United States became a party to the Berne Convention on October 31, 1988. This treaty prohibits a signatory nation from requiring a copyright notice to be placed on a work as a condition for copyright protection. The U.S. Copyright Law was therefore amended effective March 1, 1989, to permit copyright protection without notice. It must be emphasized, however, that it is still prudent to use the notice for certain international protections (U.C.C.) and to prevent any innocent infringement.

Errors in or Omission of a Copyright Notice

Failure to give copyright notice or publishing an erroneous notice had very serious consequences under the old law. Under the 1909 Act, the copyright was lost if the wrong name appeared in the notice. If the creator sold the copyright and recorded the sale, either the creator's or the new owner's name could be used. But if the sale was not recorded with the Copyright Office, use of the subsequent owner's name in the notice destroyed the copyright.

Under the 1976 Act, a mistake in the name appearing in the notice is not fatal to the copyright. However, an infringer who was honestly misled by the incorrect name could use this as a defense to a suit for copyright infringement if the proper name was not on record with the Copyright Office. This is obviously another incentive for registering a sale or license of a copyright with the Copyright Office.

Under the 1909 Act, a mistake in the year of the first publication also could have serious consequences. If an earlier date was used, the copyright term would be measured from that year, thereby decreasing the duration of protection. If a later date was used, the copyright was forfeited and the work entered the public domain. But because of the harsh consequences of losing a copyright, a mistake of one year was not penalized.

Under the 1976 Act, using an earlier date will not be of any consequence when the duration of the copyright is determined by the author's life. When the duration of the copyright is determined by the date of first publication, as in the case of a composite work or work for hire, the earlier date will be used to measure how long the copyright will last. If a later year is used, the work is considered to have been published without notice and is governed by section 405 if published prior to March 1, 1989.

The 1909 Act contained complicated rules for the proper placement of the copyright notice within the work. Improper placement was one more error that was fatal to the copyright. Although the 1976 Act, as amended, no longer requires notice, it is still a good idea to use it whenever possible. Copyright notice, if used, can appear on either the face or back of a photograph or on the cardboard frame of a transparency.

Under the 1976 Act, if a work was published between January 1, 1978 and March 1, 1989, without notice, the copyright owner is still protected for five years. If during those five years the owner registers the copyright with the Copyright Office and makes a reasonable effort to place a notice on copies of the photograph that were published without notice and distributed within the United States, full copyright protection will be granted for the appropriate duration of the published work. To place a notice on copies no longer in your possession, notify agencies, stores, or owners about the oversight and send out enough adhesive stickers for them to attach to all copies with the copyright information. If the notice has been omitted only from a relatively small number of copies, the owner need not register at all. However, risk of loss of copyright is not worth the gamble on how many copies constitute a "relatively small number." If there is any doubt, the photographer should register and attempt to get the omitted notice placed on copies that do not contain it.

A copyright owner is forgiven for an omission of notice if the omission was in violation of a contract that gave someone else the right to publish but required inclusion of the proper notice as a condition of publishing. (In other words, the copyright holder had fulfilled the responsibility for notice and is not held responsible for the other person's oversight.) Also, if the notice is removed or obliterated by an unauthorized person, this will have no effect on the validity of the copyright.

Since the purpose of the notice is to inform members of the public that the copyright owner possesses the exclusive rights granted by the statute, it is logical that someone who infringes these rights should not be penalized if the error was made because of the absence of the notice. In some cases, the infringer may be compelled to give up any profits made from the infringement. On the other hand, if the infringer has made a sizable investment for future production, the court may compel the copyright owner to grant a license to the infringer. Even though notice is not required after March 1, 1989, its use will deprive a copier of the ability to argue that an infringement was innocent.

Deposit and Registration

While a copyright notice on a photograph tells viewers who holds the copyright, it does not constitute official notice to the United States government. Once a photograph has been published, *depositing the work* and *registering an application for copyright* must be taken care of.

Depositing a work and registering an application are two different acts. Neither is a prerequisite for creating a federal copyright; as a general rule, copyright protection is automatic when an idea is "fixed in a tangible medium of expression," and, because of the copyright notice, copyright protection remains with the work after it is published or distributed to the public.

The obvious question, then, is why bother to deposit the work and file the application? As will be seen later, registration is required as a prerequisite to filing a lawsuit and may be necessary in order for you to obtain certain copyright remedies.

Under the *deposit section* of the new law, the owner of the copyright or the owner of the exclusive right of publication (usually a publisher or advertiser) must deposit in the Copyright Office, for the use of the Library of Congress, two copies of the "best edition" of the work within three months after the work has been published. In the case of an unpublished work, or a collective work, only one copy need be deposited. The copies or copy should be sent to the Register of Copyrights, Library of Congress, Washington, D.C. 20559. This basic deposit requirement also applies to works published abroad when such works are either imported into the United States or become part of an American publication.

If the two copies are not deposited within the requisite three-month period, the Register of Copyrights may demand them. (The Register of Copyrights is not omniscient; the office would know that a particular photograph had been published because of other correspondence with a publisher. If you have published a photograph on your own and never corresponded with the office, it is not likely that this demand will be made.) If the copies are not submitted within three months after demand, the person upon whom demand was made may be subject to a fine of up to $250 for each unsubmitted work. In addition, such person or persons may be required to pay the Library of Congress an amount equal to the retail cost of the work, or, if no retail cost has been established, the costs incurred by the library in acquiring the work, provided such costs are reasonable. Finally, a copyright proprietor who willfully and repeatedly refuses to comply with a demand may be liable for an additional fine of $2,500.

Depositing copies under the deposit section of the new law is not a condition of copyright protection, but in light of the penalty provisions, it would be foolish not to comply.

The *registration section* of the 1976 act requires that the copyright proprietor complete an application form, obtained from the Register of Copyrights, Library of Congress, Washington, D.C. 20559, and pay a ten-dollar registration fee. *The form is brief and straightforward; the instructions accompanying it are short and easy to understand.* In addition, the proprietor must deposit two copies of the "best edition" of the work to be registered.

In other words, to satisfy the government and assure yourself that your work is protected, *you simply fill out the form and send it, along with the required number of copies of the work and the $10 filing fee, to the Register of Copyrights.* That is it.

The process of registering a photograph for copyright is simple. The proper form is called form VA, which is the form used to register all works in the visual arts, and which may be obtained from the Copyright Office in Washington, D.C., 20559. To register the copyright in a photograph, the photographer should fill in the form and send two copies of the photograph (one copy if the photograph is unpublished) and a ten-dollar fee to the Copyright Office in Washington, D.C. The photographer must write a title on each picture. If you have many pic-

tures whose copyright you wish to register, you can save time and money by registering and copyrighting them as a single group and, rather than titling each photograph, titling the group. The title need not be impressive; it can be as simple as "1988 photographs." All works in the group must be created in the same year and if published must have been published together. It is also essential that the images be clear and the assemblage have a sufficiently orderly form and consistency of theme to bear a single title. Because internal rules of the Copyright Office are subject to change, a photographer is wise to check with the office as to what constitutes currently acceptable bulk registration practices. Bulk filings of published works may be subject to stricter requirements than bulk filings of unpublished works.

As an alternative to bulk filing in group form, the photographer could print many negatives on a single contact sheet and thus register the copyright in all of the photos on the single sheet for the cost of only one registration. Again, each photo need not be separately titled as long as the contact sheet includes an appropriate title.

Once a work has been registered as unpublished it does not need to be registered again when published. Often, a photograph's first public appearance is as part of a copyrighted collective work such as a book or magazine. If, as is usually the case, the author or publisher of the collective work and the photographer intend that the photographer will own the copyright in the photographs, the photographer can register the copyright directly on form VA. However, the photographer must file a copy of the entire collective work in which the photograph appears. Also, a large collection of one photographer's contributions to various collective works can be registered under a single application if all the work was published within a twelve-month period, each piece appeared in the collective works with a normal copyright notice in the photographer's name, and a copy of each collective work is deposited with the application. In order to accomplish this type of bulk registration, the photographer must complete a form and then list each photograph separately on a GR/CP form.

There is an alternative method of protecting photographs that appear in separately copyrighted collective works. The publisher of the collective work and the photographer may choose to view the publisher as holding the copyright to the photographs, subject to a contractual obligation to assign the copyright to the photographer. This assignment should be executed in writing and filed with the Copyright Office. The advantage of using the assignment process to establish the photographer's copyright is that there is no need for the photographer to submit a copy of the collective work or a copy of the photograph to the Copyright Office. This method presupposes that the collective work was deposited and registered by the publisher before the photographer registered the assignment.

Although registration is not a condition to copyright protection, the 1976 Act specifies that the copyright owner cannot bring a lawsuit to enforce his or her copyright until the copyright has been registered. Additionally, if the copyright is registered after an infringement occurs, the owner's legal remedies will be limited. If the copyright was registered prior to the infringement, the owner may be entitled to more complete remedies, including attorney's fees and statutory damages. No remedies will be lost if registration is made within three months of publication. Thus, the owner of a copyright has a strong incentive to register the copyright at the earliest possible time, certainly within the three-month grace period.

Proof of Registry and Copyright

You will know your registration and copyright have been accepted when the Copyright Office returns the form you submitted with a registration number on it. Probably there will be no accompanying information and it may look informal; nevertheless this will be an official document, to be stored in a safe place.

Copyright Infringement and Remedies

A copyright infringement occurs any time an unauthorized person exercises any of the exclusive rights protected by a copyright. The fact that the infringing party did not intend to improperly use protected rights or did not know that the work was protected by copyright is relevant only with respect to the penalty. All actions for infringement of copyright must be brought in a federal court within three years of the date of the infringement. The copyright owner must prove that the work was copyrighted and registered, that the infringer had access to and used the copyrighted work, and that the infringer copied a "substantial and material" portion of the copyrighted work. In order to demonstrate the extent of the damage caused by the infringement, the copyright owner must also provide evidence that shows how widely the infringing copies were distributed.

The copyright owner must prove that the infringer had access to the protected work, because an independent creation of an identical work is not an infringement. However, infringement can occur even if an entire work was not copied because any unauthorized copying of a substantial portion of a work constitutes an infringement.

Obviously, direct reproduction of a photograph without the copyright holder's permission constitutes infringement. Less obviously, a drawing or painting based entirely on a copyrighted photograph constitutes an infringement. Also, a photographer who purposely and intentionally imitates and copies the copyrighted photograph of another is guilty of infringing the copyright. Photographers should be aware that in certain circumstances they may be liable for infringing copyrights of pictures they shot themselves. In *Gross v. Seligman*, the court held that a photographer infringed the copyright owned by a publisher of a photograph the same photographer had taken earlier; when the photographer reshot the same model in a similar pose, infringement occurred. (The court noted that the later picture differed from the earlier only in that the model was older and had more wrinkles.)

If the expression of ideas, rather than simply the ideas alone, is found to be similar, the court must decide whether the similarity is substantial. This is done in two steps. First, the court looks at the more general similarities of the works, such as subject matter, setting, materials used, and the like. Expert testimony may be offered here. The second step involves a subjective judgment of the works' intrinsic similarity: Would a lay observer recognize that the alleged copy had been appropriated from the copyrighted work? No expert testimony is allowed in making this determination.

A case in the late '80s, *Hogan v. Macmillan, Inc.*, holds that the substantial similarity test applies even when the allegedly infringing material is in a different medium. George Balanchine choreographed "The Nutcracker" ballet and his estate receives royalties every time the ballet is performed. Macmillan prepared for publication a book of photographs which included sixty color pictures of scenes from a performance of "The Nutcracker." In determining whether this constituted infringement, the court of appeals noted that the correct test is whether "the ordinary observer, unless he set out to detect the disparities, would be disposed to overlook them, and regard their aesthetic appeal as the same." Furthermore, the court noted, "Even a small amount of the original, if it is qualitatively significant, may be sufficient to be an infringement, although the full original could not be recreated from the excerpt."

Even before the trial, the copyright owner may be able to obtain a preliminary court order against an infringer. The copyright owner can petition the court to seize all copies of the alleged infringing work and the negatives that produced them. To do this, the copyright owner must file a sworn statement that the work is an infringement and provide a substantial bond approved by the court. After the seizure, the alleged infringer has a chance to object to the amount or form of the bond.

After the trial, if the work is held to be an infringement, the court can order the destruction of all copies and negatives, and enjoin future infringement. In addition, the copyright owner may be awarded damages. The copyright owner may request that the court award *actual damages* or *statutory damages*—a choice that can be made any time before the final judgment is recorded. Actual damages are either the amount of the financial injury sustained by the copyright owner or, as in most cases, the equivalent of the profits made by the infringer. In proving the infringer's profits, the copyright owner need only establish the gross revenues received for the illegal exploitation of the work. The infringer then must prove any deductible expenses.

The second option is statutory damages. The amount of statutory damages is decided by the court, within specified limits: no less than $500 and no more than $20,000. The maximum possible recovery is increased to $100,000 if the copyright owner proves that the infringer knew that an illegal act was being committed. The minimum possible recovery is reduced to $200 if the infringer proves ignorance of the fact that the work was copyrighted. The court has the option to award the prevailing party its costs and attorneys' fees. As previously noted, statutory damages and attorneys' fees may not be awarded in cases where the copyright was not registered prior to infringement, provided such infringement occurred more than three months after the copyrighted work was published.

The U.S. Justice Department can criminally prosecute a copyright infringer. If the prosecutor proves beyond a reasonable doubt that the infringement was committed willfully and for commercial gain, the infringer can be fined up to $10,000 and sentenced to jail for up to one year. There is also a fine of up to $2,500 for fraudulently placing a false copyright notice on a work, for removing or obliterating a copyright notice, or for knowingly making a false statement in an application for a copyright.

Fair Use

Not every copying of a protected work will constitute an infringement. There are two basic types of non-infringing use: *fair use* and *exempted use*.

The Copyright Act of 1976 recognizes that copies of a protected work "for purposes such as criticism, comment, news reporting, teaching (including multiple copies for classroom use), scholarship or research" can be considered fair use and therefore not an infringement. However, this list is not intended to be complete nor is it intended as a definition of fair use. Fair use, in fact, is not defined by the Act. Instead, the Act cites four factors to be considered in determining whether a particular use is or is not fair:

1. The purpose and character of the use, including whether it is for commercial use or for nonprofit educational purposes,
2. The nature of the copyrighted work,
3. The amount and substantiality of the portion used in relation to the copyrighted work as a whole,
4. The effect of the use upon the potential market for, or value of, the copyrighted work.

The Act does not rank these four factors, nor does it exclude other factors in determining the question of fair use. In effect, all that the Act does is leave the doctrine of fair use to be developed by the courts.

A classic example of fair use would be reproduction of one photograph from a photography book in a newspaper or magazine review of that book. Another would be the photographing of a copyrighted photograph as background.

Fair Use in the Video Industry

The first U.S. Supreme Court case to address the fair use doctrine under the Copyright Revision Act of 1976 was *Sony Corporation of America v. Universal Studios, Inc., et al.*, in 1985. This case deals with the effect of home video recorders on copyrighted movies aired on TV, and it is an important step in defining the bounds of the fair use doctrine under the new law. Universal Studios sued Sony because Sony manufactures and sells home videotape recorders which are used to record copyrighted works shown on television. In a five-to-four decision, the Court stated that home video recording for noncommercial purposes is a fair use of copyrighted television programs.

The Supreme Court's analysis of fair use emphasized the economic consequences of home video recording to copyright owners. The Court looked to the first of the four factors listed in the 1976 Copyright Act as relevant to the fair use defense: "The purpose and character of the use." Consideration of this factor, reasoned the Court, requires a weighing of the commercial or nonprofit character of the activity. If the recorders had been used to make copies for commercial or profit-making purposes, the use would be unfair. But since video recording of television programs for private home use is a noncommercial, nonprofit activity, the court found that the use was a fair use.

The Court then considered "the effect of the use upon the potential market for or value of the copyrighted work," the fourth factor listed in the Act. Here, the Court found that although copying for noncommercial reasons may impair the copyright holder's ability to get the rewards Congress intended, to forbid a use that has no demonstrable effect upon the potential market, or upon the value of the work, would merely prohibit access to ideas without any benefit.

The rule emerging here is that a challenge to noncommercial use of a copyrighted work requires proof that the use (1) is harmful to the copyright owner or (2) would adversely affect the potential market for the copyrighted work should the use become widespread. In *Sony*, the Court concluded that Universal Studios had failed to prove actual or probable harm, and thus the recordings constituted fair use.

In this case, the alleged copyright infringement was the unauthorized recording or copying of the movies by home viewers. Several other recent video cases involve a slightly different situation: members of the public viewing video movies in what is alleged to be an unauthorized public performance. At least one lower court has held that copyright is not infringed when guests at a resort are allowed to rent video discs and view them in their rooms. However, two other courts have held that copyright is infringed when owners of video rental stores provide viewing rooms where members of the public can view the movies they have rented. The primary issue in all of these cases was whether the uses constituted public performances, not whether the

uses were fair. Nevertheless, like the *Sony* case, they illustrate the difficult copyright issue presented by the video industry. Clearly this area of the law is still developing, and any photographer connected with the video market should consult with a lawyer to learn the extent of the photographer's control over his or her work.

Historic Information

The 1968 case of *Time Inc. v. Bernard Geis Associates* involved one Abraham Zapruder of Dallas, Texas who took home movies of President Kennedy's arrival in Dallas. Zapruder started the film as the motorcade approached; when the assassination occurred, he caught it all. Zapruder had three copies made of this film; two he gave to the Secret Service solely for government use; one he sold to *Life* magazine. *Life* registered a copyright to the films and refused to allow publisher Bernard Geis Associates the right to use pictures from the film in a book. When the publisher reproduced frames in the film by charcoal sketches, *Life* sued for copyright infringement. The court found, however, that the publisher's use of the pictures was a fair use and outside the limits of copyright protection, reasoning that the public had an interest in having the fullest possible information available on the murder of President Kennedy. The court also noted that the book would have had intrinsic merit and salability without the pictures and that the publisher had offered to pay *Life* for its permission to use the pictures. The court also noted that *Life* sustained no injury because the publisher was not in competition with it.

Parody

Another area in which the fair use defense has been used successfully is in cases involving parody or burlesque. The courts have generally been sympathetic to the parodying of copyrighted works, often permitting incorporation of a substantial portion of a protected work. The test has traditionally been whether the amount copied exceeded that which was necessary to recall or "conjure up" in the mind of the viewers the work being parodied or burlesqued. In these cases the substantiality of the copy, and particularly the conjuring up test, may be more important than the factor of economic harm to the copyright proprietor. *Walt Disney Productions v. Air Pirates* involved publication of two magazines of cartoons entitled "Air Pirates Funnies" in which characters resembling Mickey and Minnie Mouse, Donald Duck, the Big Bad Wolf and the Three Little Pigs were depicted as active members of a freethinking, promiscuous, drug-ingesting counterculture. The court held that a parodist's First Amendment rights and desire to make the best parody must be balanced against the rights of the copyright owner and the protection of the owner's original expression. The judges explained that the balance is struck by giving the parodist the right to make a "copy" that is just accurate enough to conjure up the original. Since the Disney cartoon characters had widespread public recognition, a fairly inexact copy would have been sufficient to call them to mind to members of the viewing public. The court held that by copying the cartoon characters in their entirety, the defendants took more than what was necessary to place firmly in the reader's mind the parodied work and those specific attributes that were to be satirized.

Photocopying

One area in which the limits of fair use are hotly debated is the area of photocopying. The Copyright Act provides, remember, that "reproduction in copies ... for purposes such as criticism, comment, news reporting, teaching (including multiple copies for classroom use), scholarship or research" *can* be a fair use, which leaves many questions. Reproduction of what? A piece of an image? Over half an image? An image no longer generally available? How many copies? To help answer these questions, several interested organizations drafted a set of guidelines for classroom copying in nonprofit educational institutions. These guidelines are not a part of the Copyright Act but are printed in the Act's legislative history. Even though the writers of the guidelines defined the guide as "minimum standards of educational fair use," major educational groups have publicly expressed the fear that publishers would attempt to establish the guidelines as maximum standards beyond which there could be no fair use.

As all this demonstrates, it is not easy to define what sorts of uses are fair uses. Questions continue to be resolved on a case-by-case basis. Thus, a photographer should consult a lawyer where it appears that one of his works has been infringed or where the photographer intends to use someone else's copyrighted work. The lawyer can research what the courts have held in cases with similar facts.

Exempted Uses

In many instances the ambiguities of the fair use doctrine have been resolved by statutory exemptions. Exempted uses are those specifically permitted by

statute in situations where the public interest in making a copy outweighs any harm to the copyright proprietor.

Libraries and Archives

Perhaps the most significant of these exemptions is the library and archives exemption, which basically provides that libraries and archives may reproduce and distribute a single copy of a work provided that (1) such reproduction and distribution is not for the purpose of direct or indirect commercial gain; (2) the collections of the library or archives are available to the public or available to researchers affiliated with the library or archives as well as to others doing research in a specialized field; and (3) the reproduction and distribution of the work includes a copyright notice.

According to the legislative history of the Copyright Act, Congress particularly encourages copying of films made before 1942 because these films are printed on film stock with a nitrate base that will decompose in time. Thus, so long as an organization is attempting to preserve our cultural heritage, copying of old films is allowed and encouraged under the fair use doctrine.

The exemption for libraries and archives is intended to cover only single copies of a work. It does not generally cover multiple reproductions of the same material, whether made on one occasion or over a period of time, and whether intended for use by one person or for separate use by the individual members of a group. Under interlibrary arrangements, various libraries may provide one another with works missing from their respective collections, unless these distribution arrangements substitute for a subscription or purchase of a given work.

This exemption in no way affects the applicability of fair use, nor does it apply where such copying is prohibited in contractual arrangements agreed to by the library or archives when it obtained the work.

Sovereign Immunity

A number of comparatively recent cases have involved the question of whether or not the federal government or any state can be liable for copyright infringement. Thus far, because of the doctrine of *sovereign immunity*, federal and state governments have been found to be protected against liability for infringement when using copyrighted work. Since the United States government or a state government can only be sued when it consents to be sued, the plaintiff must establish that the government authorized or consented to the infringement and that the government agreed to be sued for it.

The Eleventh Amendment to the United States Constitution has been used to shield states from liability for copyright infringement when they did not waive their immunity. Thus, a photographer may have work infringed by the state or federal government and have no redress. The immunity, however, may not extend to the individual responsible for the infringement. The United States Court of Appeals for the Fourth Circuit has held that the Eleventh Amendment may shield a state university from liability for copyright infringement, but the publication director who used the infringing photo in the student catalogue may herself be liable.

Chapter 2

DEFAMATION AND LIBEL

In the year 400 B.C., the Greek philosopher Socrates was convicted of teaching atheism to the children of Athens and was sentenced to death. Of the four hundred jurors, all but two voted for conviction. In his defense, Socrates claimed that most of the charges were based on lies and that his reputation had been unjustly attacked for years. For example, he argued, in *The Clouds*, a play by Aristophanes that was performed before the entire population of Athens, the bumbling teacher of philosophy was named Socrates. However, in Athens free speech was an absolute right, and Socrates had no protection against statements which today would be considered defamatory.

Despite the First Amendment guarantee that freedom of speech will not be abridged, in contemporary America that freedom is limited. Defamatory material which includes photographs is not absolutely protected — and is in fact prohibited by law in all fifty states. A statement will generally be considered defamatory if it tends to subject a person to hatred, contempt, or ridicule or if it results in injury to that person's reputation while in office, in business, or at work.

The American Law Institute defines libel as publication of defamatory matter "by written or printed words, by its embodiment in physical form (such as in photographs), or by any other form of communication which has the potentially harmful qualities characteristic of written or printed words." Photographs can also be defamatory. Generally, a picture by itself cannot be the basis for liability because truth is a defense to libel and the camera merely records what is there. However, photographs can become defamatory if they are airbrushed or otherwise altered in a way that exposes the subject to ridicule or contempt.

Photographs usually are published with accompanying text or captions. In determining whether or not a photograph is defamatory, the court will consider a publication in its entirety. To protect against liability for defamation, a photographer should caption photographs accurately before selling them. Also, the photographer should be careful not to participate in or explicitly approve of false text accompanying the photographs. In *Cantrell v. Forest City Publishing Co.*, a reporter wrote a story on the poverty of a family whose father had been killed in a flood. A photographer took fifty pictures of the family's home, some of which were published with the story. When the family sued for invasion of privacy, the photographer was not held liable because there was no evidence that he was involved in writing the text.

If defamation is written or tangible, it is libel; if it is oral, it is *slander*. For the most part the same laws and principles govern all defamatory statements, but since a photographer's liability involves images that appear on paper, we will focus here on libel. As a photographer, you must be cautious about any photographs or captions that might be considered defamatory. If the work is published — and as you will see, "published" has a very broad meaning in the context of libel — you, as the photographer, could be sued along with the publisher, under the libel statutes.

It is not always easy to determine whether a photograph is defamatory. In order to give you some idea of the scope of libel, let us take a closer look at what kinds of photographs the courts have found to be libelous. Then we will look at who can sue a photographer for libel, and various defenses a photographer can use against different plaintiffs.

Actionable Libel

Actionable libel is libel that would furnish legal grounds for a lawsuit. In order for a photograph to be libelous, it must, in legal terminology, *convey a defamatory meaning* about an identifiable person or persons, and must have been published. Thus, a photograph of, for example, a Jewish leader in which a Nazi armband has been air-brushed in would be libelous.

Courts have traditionally put libel into two categories: *libel per se* and *libel per quod*. In libel per se the defamatory meaning is apparent from the statement or thing itself. In libel per quod, the defamatory meaning is conveyed only in conjunction with other material. In libel per quod, the photograph may be susceptible to more than one reasonable interpretation, but as long as any one of the interpretations is defamatory, the picture will be libelous.

Libel Per Se

One example of libel per se is an accusation of criminal or morally reprehensible acts. An accusation of criminal conduct is libelous per se even though it is not explicitly stated; if the photographer has published a photograph and captions that describe a crime or has cast suspicion by innuendo, that is sufficient for libel per se. In *Ragano v. Time, Inc.*, the court found potential defamation liability based on publication of a photograph of seven men seated at a restaurant table accompanied by an article that referred to the men, two of whom were attorneys, as Cosa Nostra hoodlums. Similarly, in *Hagler v. Democrat News*, Inc., a newspaper ran a photograph of a couple's beach cabin to illustrate an article on a drug raid. Because the photograph included a sign identifying the owners of the cabin, the owners sued for invasion of privacy and for defamation. As the pictured cabin was in no way implicated in the drug raid, the photograph would indeed have been defamatory had the text of the article not made it clear that the drug raid occurred in another cabin.

On the other hand, it is never libel per se to say that someone is exercising a legal right—even though the person may not want the fact known. For example, it is not libel per se to say or to imply by a photograph that a man killed someone in self-defense, that he brought a divorce suit against his wife, or that he invoked the Fifth Amendment forty times. Although these statements may cast suspicion, they cannot be libelous per se because they merely report the exercise of a legal right.

To state that someone has a loathsome or contagious disease such as syphilis, gonorrhea, or AIDS is libelous per se. A statement that describes deviant sexual conduct or unchastity, particularly by a woman, is libelous per se. In *Esposito v. Cinema X Magazine*, the court found that publication of a woman's nude photograph, without her consent, in a magazine that promoted the careers of aspiring porn stars was defamatory. The suggestion of unwed pregnancy also undermines a woman's reputation for chastity and can be the basis for defamation action. In *Triangle Publications, Inc. v. Chumley*, a newspaper and magazine published a photograph of a teen-age girl embracing a man and a photograph of her alleged diary with an entry stating she was pregnant. These photos were part of an advertisement for a television series on teen pregnancy. The court held that the photographs were defamatory.

When the statement involves politics, the determination of libel per se is more difficult. Today, courts generally agree that a statement that a person belongs to a particular political group will be libel per se only if that group advocates the use of violence as a means of achieving political ends. Thus, to say that someone belongs to the Ku Klux Klan would probably be libel per se. But to say that someone is a racist would probably not be, since racism is not necessarily intertwined with the use of violence. In some instances, though, a photograph that makes a statement concerning someone's political affiliation may constitute libel per se regardless of the political group's attitude toward violence. For example, to depict someone as a communist may be libel per se because communist affiliation is generally injurious to a person's reputation within significant portions of society today.

It is usually deemed libel per se to impute to a professional person a breach of professional ethics, general unfitness or inefficiency. For example, it may be libel per se to indicate that a person's business is bankrupt, because the statement implies a general unfitness to do business. However, to indicate that the business person did not pay a certain debt is not libel per se, because everyone has a legal right to contest a debt. Similarly, it may be libel per se to imply that a doctor is a butcher, because it implies general incompetence. But it is not libel per se to imply that the doctor made a mistake, so long as it does not imply general incompetence. Everyone makes mistakes.

There is a gray area concerning statements or pictures about certain business practices that may not be illegal but which nonetheless could give a business bad publicity. To indicate someone is cutting prices would not be libel per se, but to indicate someone is cutting prices to drive a competitor out of business would be.

It is impossible to describe every situation that could constitute libel per se, since any situation can be libel per se if it is likely to produce a reprehensible opinion of someone in the minds of a large number of reasonable people. Remember, the rule of thumb is that a photograph or statement is libelous per se when the defamatory meaning is clear from the situation itself.

Libel per Quod

In libel per quod, since the defamatory meaning is conveyed only in conjunction with other factors, the plaintiff who sues for libel must introduce the context of the situation and demonstrate to the court how the picture and caption, text, or other pictures as a whole result in a defamatory innuendo. For example, *Gomes v. Fried* involved a photograph that showed an officer sitting in his police car with his head tilted to one side, and it was accompanied by a caption reading: "Officer Gomes' car shown in the center of the lightly traveled Bristol Avenue (Sunday afternoon) prowling for traffic violations. His head tilted may suggest something." While the officer admitted that the photograph was accurate, the court observed that the innuendo in the caption made it potentially defamatory, suggesting to ordinary readers that the officer was sleeping on duty. In fact, as many readers stated in later letters to the newspaper, and as the officer himself testified, he was called "Sleepy" and known as the Sleeping Officer. Nevertheless, the codefendants, the editor and publisher of the newspaper, knew that the officer was not sleeping, but was writing a traffic citation at the time the photograph was taken. Thus, although the photograph was accurate, the court held that the photograph could be the basis for a suit.

Defamatory Advertising and Trade Libel

Photographers should be aware that they are potentially liable for a type of defamation known as *trade libel* if they help to create advertisements that impugn the quality of commercial merchandise or products. If an advertisement reflects adversely on a competitor's character, it can constitute defamation per se. If the advertisement on its face implies that a competitor is fraudulent or dishonest, and if the competitor can prove financial loss, she may have an action for defamation per quod.

Proof of Damage

The distinction between libel per se and libel per quod is important primarily because it determines whether the plaintiff has to prove damage. Where there is libel per se, damage to reputation will be presumed and the plaintiff need not prove it. If, however, the charge is libel per quod, damage normally must be proved, although there are some exceptions to this general rule. If the innuendo in the libel per quod falls within one of four categories, damage will be presumed as in libel per se. The four categories are innuendos that (1) adversely reflect upon someone's ability to conduct a business, trade or profession, (2) impute unchastity to an unmarried woman, (3) accuse someone of committing a crime of moral turpitude,* or (4) accuse someone of having a loathsome disease such as leprosy or a venereal disease.

Publication

As mentioned earlier, a photograph must be published in order to constitute actionable libel. The legal meaning of *publication* in the libel context is very broad. Once a photograph is communicated to a third person who sees and understands it, the photograph, in the eyes of the law, has been published. Thus, if you show a photograph to someone other than the subject, you have published the photograph.

Generally, the person who is defamed can bring a separate lawsuit for each repetition of the defamatory photograph. However, when the photograph is contained in a book, magazine, or newspaper, a majority of courts have adopted what is known as the *single-publication rule.* Under this rule, a person cannot make each copy of the book grounds for a separate suit. Rather, the number of copies is taken into account only for purposes of determining the extent of damages.

Who Can Sue for Libel?

In order for someone to sue for libel, the photograph at issue must clearly depict or identify that person or entity. This is easy to prove, of course, when the plaintiff is identified by name in the text or caption or where the plaintiff is clearly visible and identifiable in the photograph. But if a plaintiff is not identified by name, the plaintiff can prove that he or she was nonetheless "identified" by showing that a third party could reasonably infer that the photograph was of the plaintiff.

The courts have uniformly held that groups, corporations and partnerships can sue for libel just as an individual can. Although there has been disagreement among the states as to whether not-for-profit

---

*A crime of moral turpitude is something that is immoral in itself, irrespective of the fact that it is punished by law. Examples are rape and murder.

corporations should be protected, the trend seems to be to allow nonprofit corporations to sue when they are injured in their ability to collect or distribute funds.

If a defamatory picture is published depicting an identified group of people, the possibility of each member of that group having a good cause of action will depend on the size of the group and whether the photograph defames all or only a part of the group.

Where the group is composed of more than one hundred members, the individuals generally do not have a good cause of action. If, for example, someone publishes a photograph of thousands of people in a ball park audience and added a caption indicating that all depicted were thieves, it is unlikely that one person's reputation could be damaged as a result of the photograph. On the other hand, if that same caption described a small group of individuals in the photograph, those individuals could probably win a defamation suit, since they would be more likely to be subject to contempt, hatred, or ridicule as a result of the defamatory picture.

The individual members of a group might not prevail if the allegedly defamatory statement referred only to a portion of the group. If, for example, someone states that "some members" of a particular trade group shown in a photograph "are communists," the individual members probably cannot prevail in a defamation suit, since the statement is not all-inclusive, and since those included are not named. Again, the size of the group could affect the court's ruling. If the partially defamed group is small and the people are recognizable, it would be more likely that the reputation of each member had been damaged, even though the statement was not all-inclusive.

A photographer confronted with the question of whether or not to publish a work that identifies a person, group, or entity should make a two-step analysis. First, does the picture defame a reputation? If the answer is no, then it may be safely published (assuming no other form of liability such as copyright infringement or invasion of privacy is involved). If the answer is yes, the second step is to determine whether there is a valid defense.

Defenses to Libel

Since photographers often write captions or descriptions to accompany their photographs, you as a photographer need to know the situations in which you can defend your right to publish certain kinds of pictures. Even if a plaintiff proves defamation, publication, and damages (where damages must be proved), the photographer may nevertheless prevail in a lawsuit if he or she is able to establish a valid defense.

Truth

Truth is an absolute defense to a charge of defamation, although it may not protect against other charges such as invasion of privacy. It is not necessary for a potentially defamatory statement to be correct in every respect in order to be considered true. As long as the statement is true in all essential particulars, the defense will be acceptable. For example, if the caption "X robbed Bank A" appeared under a photograph of a bank robbery, it would be considered true, and therefore not actionable, even though the photograph was in fact of a robbery of Bank B. The essential fact is that X was guilty of robbing a bank, so it is irrelevant which bank was robbed.

Opinion

A second possible defense is that the supposedly defamatory material was one of *opinion* rather than fact. The rationale for this defense is that one's opinion can never be false, and therefore cannot be defamatory. Of course, the line between a statement of fact and an opinion is often hard to draw, particularly in the area of literary or artistic criticism.

Not surprisingly, art, literary, and drama critics have frequently been accused of libel after they have published particularly scathing reviews. When criticizing the work of artists, the critic is free to use rhetorical hyperbole as long as the statements do not reflect on the character of the artist. For example, in the early '70s Gore Vidal sued William F. Buckley, Jr., for calling Vidal's book *Myra Breckenridge* pornography. The court held that, in context, the statement did not assail Vidal's character by suggesting that he himself was a pornographer. Thus the statement was not defamatory.

An example of criticism that did assail character is a famous case from the 1890s, in which the American artist James Whistler won a defamation suit against John Ruskin, the English art critic. In his assessment of Whistler's painting "Nocturne in Brown and Gold," Ruskin wrote: "I have seen, and heard, much of Cockney impudence before now, but never expected to hear a coxcomb ask 200 guineas for flinging a pot of paint in the public's face." On the surface, this statement was an expression of opinion of the painting's worth. At the same time it implied facts about Whistler's motives, suggesting that he was defrauding the public by charging money for something that was not even art. The court found these implied facts to be defamatory since they described Whistler as unfit professionally.

If an opinion concerns a topic of public interest, it *might* be allowed, since such opinions do have some, if limited, privilege. Such a situation arose in *Lavin v. New York News, Inc.*, when a court declined to find that a photograph of two policemen captioned "Best Cops Money Can Buy" constituted defamation. The court held that the photograph and the accompanying article on organized crime came within the privilege concerning opinions on subjects of public interest.

Consent

Someone accused of defamation may also raise the defense of *consent*. It is not libelous to publish a photograph of a person who has consented to its publication. In this situation, the extent of the material that may be legally published is governed by the terms and context of the consent.

An interesting case that turned on what constitutes consent concerned a student humor magazine that had run a piece for Mother's Day consisting of four pictures. One picture was totally black. Under it was the caption "Father Loves Mother." Another picture showed a little girl with the caption "Daughter Loves Mother (And wants to be one too!)." A third picture showed a boy whose arm was tattooed with a heart enclosing the word *Mother* captioned "Sailor Boy Loves Mother," and the final picture showed a face partly covered by a hood, labeled "Midwife Loves Mother." The picture of the little girl happened to be a photograph of the daughter of a local Methodist minister, a Mr. Langford, and it was rumored that he was about to sue the school newspaper for libel. Langford maintained that the pictures and captions made innuendos about the unchastity of his daughter, his wife, and himself. Another student newspaper sent two reporters to interview the minister, and he gladly consented to the interview. When the minister filed suit, the newspaper that had conducted the interview published an article which truthfully set out the facts of the suit and contained material from the interview. It also republished the allegedly libelous material. The minister then sued the second paper, but he lost because the court found that he had consented to republication of the material.

Reports of Official Proceedings

Another defense to what would otherwise be considered defamation is that the statement or picture was part of a *report of official proceedings* or a *public meeting*. As long as the context is a "fair and accurate" account of those proceedings, there can be no liability, even if the picture in question is both defamatory and false. The requirement that the publication be fair and accurate means that whatever was published must be a fair and balanced rendition. For example, a writer may not quote only one side of an argument made in court if there was also a rebuttal to that argument. The account need not be an exact quote, and it is permissible to include some background material to put an accompanying photograph into proper perspective. However, a photographer or caption-writer must be careful not to include extraneous information such as editorial comments (which are themselves defamatory), because these will not be protected by the report of official proceedings defense.

Photographers and lawyers learned long ago that it is not always clear what constitutes an official proceeding or public meeting. Court proceedings from arrest to conviction are definitely official proceedings. On the other hand, photographs taken outside of court are not. A newsletter sent by a legislator to constituents does not generally constitute an official proceeding, whereas a political convention probably does.

Reply

Another defense to an accusation of libel is that of *reply*. If someone is defamed, that person is privileged to reply, even if the first person is defamed in the process. This privilege is limited to the extent that the reply may not exceed the provocation. For example, if A publishes a photograph of B and indicates that B is a communist, B has a right to reply that A is a liar or that A is a right-wing extremist, because either of these comments bears some relation to the original defamation. If, later on, A sues B for libel because of the statement about A being a right-wing extremist, B can simply show that the statement was in response to the material published by A: the reply defense. But if B made the mistake of responding to A by calling A a thief — a statement that bears no relation to A's accusation — B cannot have recourse to the reply defense.

Statute of Limitations

Another possible defense is the *statute of limitations*. Basically, statutes of limitations limit the time period within which an injured party can sue. The reason for these time limits is the difficulty of resolving old claims once the evidence becomes stale and the witnesses forget or disappear.

In the case of libel, the injured party must generally sue within one or two years from the date of first publication, although in some states the period is longer. If suit is brought after this time has elapsed, the statute of limitations will bar the suit.

For photographs, the period of time allowed by statutes of limitations for libel begins when a photograph is first published. Since publication means the act of communicating the matter at issue to one or more persons, the first publication of a book, magazine, or newspaper containing the photograph is deemed to occur when the publisher releases the finished product for sale. A second edition is generally not considered a separate publication for calculating time elapsed under the statute of limitations, at least where the single-publication rule is followed.

Absence of Actual Malice

The defense most frequently used in recent libel suits was created by the United State Supreme Court in 1964 in *The New York Times Co. v. Sullivan*. The case against *The Times* concerned a photo advertisement it published which contained some inaccuracies and supposedly defamed L.B. Sullivan, the police chief of Montgomery, Alabama. The Supreme Court held that *The New York Times* was not guilty of libel, stating the existence of

a profound national commitment to the principle that debate on public issues should be uninhibited, robust, and wide-open, and that it may well include vehement, caustic, and sometimes unpleasantly sharp attacks on government and public officials.

Thus the Court found that the First Amendment provides some protection to writings which criticize public officials for anything they do that is in any way relevant to their official conduct.

By virtue of the First Amendment protection, or privilege, when a public official sues for defamation the official must prove with "convincing clarity" that the defendant published the statement with "actual malice." Actual malice is defined as knowledge of the falsity, or a reckless disregard for the truth or falsity, of the statements published. Reckless disregard is further defined as serious doubts about the truth of the statement. Conflicts often arise in suits against newspapers when a public official is the plaintiff and tries to find the source of a paper's information in order to show reckless disregard of the truth, while the newspaper tries to protect its source.

The *Sullivan* case placed a greater burden of proof upon public officials in defamation suits. Prior to *Sullivan*, a preponderance of the evidence was simply proof of defamation, but now the courts require "convincing clarity," which is somewhere between the "preponderance of the evidence" required in most civil suits and the "proof beyond a reasonable doubt" required in criminal cases.

For the photographer, the result of *Sullivan* was the public-official privilege—the privilege to examine public officials with considerable scrutiny.

The standards resulting from *Sullivan* were applied in 1984 in the highly publicized case of *Sharon v. Time Inc.*, which arose after the massacre of Palestinian refugees by Lebanese Phalangists in retaliation for the assassination of Lebanon's President Gemayel. At the time, Lebanon was occupied by Israeli forces and Ariel Sharon was Israel's defense minister. *Time* magazine published a story alleging that Sharon had secretly discussed the possibility of such a retaliatory attack with Gemayel's family, who remained politically powerful. Sharon sued *Time*, which steadfastly refused to retract the allegations.

The jury held that *Time*'s article was false, and that Sharon was defamed by it. But the jury also found that *Time* did not possess actual malice, which meant that the magazine did not have to pay any damages. Both sides claimed victory. Sharon declared himself vindicated of the allegations, while *Time* pointed to the fact that it did not have to pay damages to Sharon. Most commentators, however, agreed that *Time* suffered great damage to its journalistic reputation.

Ariel Sharon went on to file a second lawsuit for libel against *Time* in Israel. According to a legal treaty between the United States and Israel, judgments of Israeli courts are recognized in America and vice versa. The Tel Aviv district court judge ruled that he would accept the American jury's ruling that *Time* had defamed Sharon and printed false material about him. Significantly, it is not necessary to prove malice in a libel suit under Israeli law; it is necessary only to show that a story is false and defamatory. Consequently, *Time*'s Israeli lawyer was reported as stating that the magazine had little chance of winning in the Israeli court.

In January of 1986, while the Tel Aviv judge was in the process of deciding the case, the parties announced an out-of-court settlement. In return for Ariel Sharon's dropping his libel action, *Time* stated to the Tel Aviv court that the reference to Sharon's supposed conversation in Beirut was "erroneous." In addition, *Time* agreed to pay part of the Israeli minister's legal fees. The *Time* statement appeared to acknowledge more culpability than had previously been admitted. The difference in the outcomes in the two cases illustrates the importance of requiring a plaintiff to prove actual malice in a libel suit. To some extent, this requirement in American law results in broader protection for the press than exists in other countries.

The American jury's verdict in *Sharon* may have spurred a settlement in another much-publicized case being tried at the same time, *Westmoreland v. CBS*. In *Westmoreland*, the former commander of American troops in Vietnam challenged allegations of wrongdoing on his part made by CBS in a documentary about the war.

It has been speculated that the parties in *Westmoreland* realized that a verdict similar to that in Sharon would be damaging to both of them. Settlement of the case allowed both sides to claim victory without the necessity of submitting the issues to the jury.

The depth of criticism required for a finding of libel under the public-official privilege created in *Sharon* varies from case to case. The most intimate aspects of private life are fair game when one is discussing an elected official or a candidate's qualifications for political office. On the other hand, when discussing civil servants such as police and firefighters, only comments directly related to their function as civil servants are similarly privileged.

The Supreme Court has defined public officials as those "who have, or appear to the public to have, substantial responsibility for or control over the conduct of governmental affairs." This category has been held to include all civil servants from police officers to secretaries. Recently, the Court has begun applying the public-official exception to public figures as well — but it has experienced a good deal of difficulty in determining who should be considered a public figure.

A Public Figure

At present the United States Supreme Court recognizes two ways in which people may become public figures. The first is to "occupy positions of such persuasive power and influence that they are deemed public figures for all purposes." This category includes those who are frequently in the news but are not public officials, such as Henry Kissinger, Bob Dylan, and Walter Cronkite. The fact that they are deemed public figures "for all purposes" means that the scope of privileged comment about them is virtually without limit.

The second way of becoming a public figure is to "thrust [oneself] to the forefront of particular public controversies in order to influence the resolution of the issues involved." This category has two requirements. First, there must be a public controversy. The Court in *Time, Inc. v. Firestone* held that not every newsworthy event is a public controversy. Nor is an event a public controversy merely because there may be different opinions as to the propriety of an act.

The *Firestone* case is a good example of how narrowly the Court applies the term "public controversy." *Time* magazine accidentally published a story stating that Mr. Firestone was divorced from Mrs. Firestone because of "extreme cruelty and adultery." In fact, the divorce was granted because the judge found that neither party to the divorce displayed "the least susceptibility to domestication," a novel ground for divorce under Florida law. *Time* went astray because the judge himself had once commented that there was enough testimony of extramarital adventures on both sides "to make Dr. Freud's hair curl." In its defense against Mrs. Firestone's suit for libel, *Time* insisted that Mrs. Firestone was a public figure. As evidence of this, it showed that the divorce had been covered in nearly every major newspaper and that Mrs. Firestone herself had held periodic press conferences during the trial. But the Court refused to equate a *cause celebre* with a public controversy. As a result, Mrs. Firestone was required to prove only that *Time* had been negligent in its reading of the Court's opinion and that there was actual injury.

The second requirement in this public-figure category is that the person has voluntarily thrust himself or herself into the controversy in order to influence the issues. This requirement would be met if someone's actions were calculated to draw attention to that person or to arouse public sentiment, but not if the person were arrested or convicted. A student who makes a speech during a peace demonstration, say, is considered a public figure only with respect to the subject of the demonstration. In matters that have nothing to do with the political controversy, the courts would probably regard the student as a private individual.

To reiterate, the Supreme Court will require only public officials and public figures to prove actual malice in a defamation suit. Yet even private persons may have to prove negligence if they sue a newspaper for libel which occurred in a piece relating to a matter of public concern. Although the Supreme Court held that the plaintiff in *Firestone* did not have the heavy burden of proof of a public figure, she still had to prove negligence in her suit for libel. This is more difficult than that what is required of the average person who has been defamed in regard to some private, unnewsworthy matter. Generally, the everyday, private person who sues for libel does not need to prove actual malice or any other state of mind. All he or she need demonstrate to the court is that a writing, or a photo caption, identifying him or her conveyed a defamatory meaning and was published.

The Supreme Court recently increased the burden of proof for private plaintiffs suing newspapers writing matters of public concern. In *Philadelphia Newspapers, Inc. v. Hepps*, a 1986 case, a businessman operating a franchise in Philadelphia sued the Philadelphia Inquirer for publication of several articles asserting that he had links to organized crime and had used these links to influence local government. The Court held that in such a case the plaintiff, Hepps, not the defendant, will bear the burden of proof on the issue of the truth or falsity of the statement. The Court found that the Constitution requires that the burden be so shifted in order to ensure that true speech on matters of public concern not be stifled.

Court opinions seem to indicate that a private person suing a newspaper on a matter of public concern will have to prove both that there was negligence on the part of the paper, and that the information published was in fact false. How does one determine whether the information involved is of public concern? The distinction may hinge on whether or not the defendant represents the media. The Supreme Court dealt with the media-nonmedia distinction in a case involving a reporting service that published and circulated a grossly inaccurate credit report. The reporting service pleaded First Amendment protection, but the Court, by a five-to-four vote, held that since the credit report was not a matter of public concern, it was not entitled to protection by the First Amendment. Thus, the injured business had only to prove defamation and publication.

Unfortunately, the Court did not define what kind of speech or photograph *is* of public concern. Lacking such a definition, news writers and photojournalists need to be extremely careful about the subjects of their reports and pictures.

A question that has often been raised by legal scholars, but has as yet not received an answer from the courts, is whether a person who at one time was a public figure or involved in a matter of public concern can ever effectively return to private life. It is probably better to remain on the safe side and treat anyone who has been out of the limelight for more than five years as a private person.

Despite the tremendous burden of proof placed upon public officials and public figures, they are still able to win in many defamation suits. For example, Barry Goldwater was successful in his suit against Ralph Ginzburg, who had published an article which stated that Goldwater was psychotic and therefore unfit to be president. Goldwater proved that material in the article was intentionally distorted. In a later case, actress Carol Burnett won a libel suit against the *National Enquirer*. The article said that Burnett had been drunk and boisterous in a Washington restaurant when in fact her behavior had been beyond reproach. Burnett was able to show that the article was published with reckless disregard for the truth or falsity of the facts and thus satisfied the malice requirement.

Protection against Defamation Suits

Since the law on libel is complicated, and subject to continual modification by the Supreme Court, any potentially libelous work should be submitted to a lawyer before publication is considered. Remember, everyone directly involved in the publication of libelous material can be held liable. Photographers should be aware that publishers may attempt to protect themselves from defamation suits by including a clause in the photographer's contract stating that the photographer guarantees not to have libeled anyone and accepts responsibility for covering costs if the publisher is sued. The risks involved in agreeing to such a clause are obvious.

Chapter 3

THE RIGHT OF PRIVACY

The right to be protected from a wrongful invasion of privacy, largely taken for granted today, is a relatively new legal concept. In fact, the right of privacy was not suggested as a legal principle until 1890, when arguments for developing the right appeared in a *Harvard Law Review* article written by the late Justice Louis Brandeis and his law partner, Samuel Warren. This article, written largely because of excessive media attention given to the social affairs of Warren's wife, maintained that the media were persistently "overstepping in every direction the obvious bounds of propriety and of decency" in violation of the individual's right "to be let alone."

From this rather modest beginning the concept of a right to privacy began to take hold. In many of the early privacy cases the *Harvard Law Review* article was cited as justification for upholding privacy claims, although courts also found their own justifications. For example, in 1905 a Georgia court suggested that the right of privacy is rooted in natural law. In the words of the court: "The right of privacy has its foundations in the instincts of nature. It is recognized intuitively, consciousness being the witness that can be called to establish its existence." Other courts have upheld right-of-privacy laws on constitutional grounds, both state and federal, arguing that although there is no express recognition of a right to privacy in the U.S. Constitution, it can nevertheless be inferred from the combined language of the First, Fourth, Fifth, Ninth, and Fourteenth Amendments.

Although the right of privacy is now generally recognized, the precise nature of the right varies from state to state. Some states, such as New York, Oklahoma, Utah, Virginia, and California, have enacted right-of-privacy statutes. Others simply recognize the right as a matter of common law. Others—Texas, Nebraska, Rhode Island, and Wisconsin—expressly refuse to recognize a right of privacy, while still others have not yet taken a position. Because the right of privacy is not consistent throughout the states, you should keep in mind that the situations discussed in this chapter might be handled differently in the state where you live. The cases here should not be relied upon to determine a photographer's rights and liabilities. They are included simply to illustrate some of the legal developments in the area of privacy rights so that you can avoid obvious traps, identify problems as they arise, and know when to consult a lawyer.

Some of the confusion surrounding the right of privacy can be resolved by dividing the right of privacy into four specific categories: (1) intrusion upon another's seclusion, (2) public disclosure of private facts, (3) portrayal of another in a false light, and (4) commercial appropriation of another's name or likeness. These categories represent the four different types of civil invasion of privacy currently recognized by the courts.

Intrusion upon Another's Seclusion

At issue in intrusion upon another's seclusion is the extent to which a photographer intrudes upon someone's right of privacy for purposes of taking pictures to be used in combination with political, personal, or biographical commentary. An intrusion upon another's seclusion will be wrongful if three elements are present. First, there must be an actual intrusion of some sort. Second, the intrusion must be of a type that would be offensive to a reasonable person; courts will not consider the particular sensibilities of the plaintiff. Third, the intruder must have entered that which is considered someone's private domain. Thus, for example, it is generally not unlawful to take pictures of a person in a public place or disclose facts the person has discussed publicly. It is likely, however, that an intrusion would be wrongful if someone goes on someone else's land without permission or opens someone else's private desk and reads materials found there. Publication is not a necessary element in a case for intrusion since the intrusion itself is the invasion of privacy.

The nature of a wrongful intrusion upon another's seclusion is well illustrated by two cases: *Dietemann v. Time, Inc.* and *Galella v. Onassis*. In *Dietemann*, the plaintiff claimed to be a healer. Investigators for *Life* magazine sought to prove that he was in fact a charlatan. In the process of checking out his claim, reporters entered Dietemann's house under false pretenses, and while in his house they surreptitiously took pictures and recorded conversations. This information was then written up in an expose appearing in *Life*. The court held that the healer's right of privacy had indeed been violated, since there was no question that his seclusion was invaded unreasonably.

An even more obvious intrusion is illustrated by *Galella v. Onassis*. Ronald Galella is a freelance photographer specializing in photographs of celebrities, and the persistence and manner in which he performs his job are unparalleled. For a number of years Jacqueline Onassis, Caroline Kennedy, John Kennedy, Jr., and other members of the Kennedy family were among his favorite subjects. Onassis and the others were constantly confronted by Galella, who used highly offensive chase scene techniques, in parks and churches, at funeral services, theatres, schools and elsewhere. One of his practices was to shock or surprise his subjects in order to photograph them in a state of surprise. While taking these photographs, he would sometimes utter offensive or snide comments. After hearing a wealth of evidence regarding this type of behavior, the court, in a fairly scathing opinion, held that Galella had wrongfully intruded upon the seclusion of his subjects. Finding monetary damages to be an inadequate remedy, the court issued a permanent injunction that prohibited Galella from getting within a certain distance of Onassis and the others.

In both *Dietemann* and *Galella* the defendants maintained that any attempt to restrain their efforts to get information or photographs was constitutionally suspect, since it would infringe upon their First Amendment freedoms. These arguments are not particularly persuasive. Courts have universally attempted to *balance* rights in intrusion cases: The right of the press to obtain information is balanced against the equal right of the individual to enjoy privacy and seclusion. Thus, the courts have refused to construe the First Amendment as a license to steal, trespass, harass, or engage in any other conduct that would clearly be wrongful or offensive.

This balancing approach is apparent in *Galella*. The court found that the intrusions were so pervasive and offensive that it did not matter that many of the acts occurred while Onassis and her children were in public rather than private places. Their right to privacy had been significantly infringed. Furthermore, the products of Galella's efforts were trivial, being nothing more than fodder for gossip magazines. Thus, the harmful effect of suppressing his First Amendment freedoms was found to be slight or nonexistent. Significantly, the court did not forbid further photographs, but merely regulated the manner in which they could be taken.

For the dedicated photojournalist, the possibility of an intrusion suit should always be weighed against the natural tendency to aggressively pursue the facts, but even photojournalists on important assignments have no right to harass, trespass, use electronic surveillance, or enter a private domain.

Photographers should be aware that even a photograph taken in a public place can result in liability for wrongful intrusion. In *Daily Times Democrat v. Graham*, the court found wrongful intrusion when a photographer took the picture of an obese woman whose skirt was blown upward while she was standing in a fun house. Photographers should also be aware that some states have statutes that make the use of hidden cameras a misdemeanor.

Public Disclosure of Private Facts

The public disclosure of private facts was the aspect of the right of privacy that first prompted Warren and Brandeis to publish their article in the *Harvard Law Review*. Plaintiffs are less likely to win in these circumstances, however, because the First Amendment protection that modern courts apply to "newsworthy information," which includes educational or informative material, as well as current events, makes it unlikely that photographers shooting matters of public interest will incur liability for public disclosure. Where the information disclosed is true, the First Amendment freedoms afforded to the press almost invariably outweigh an individual's right of privacy. Only in very limited circumstances will the balance be shifted in favor of the individual.

In order to bring a case for this kind of invasion of privacy, the plaintiff must prove that private facts about him or her were publicly disclosed and that the disclosure would be objectionable to a person of ordinary sensibilities.

The first question, then, is whether a photograph involves private facts. This is basically a matter of common sense; anything that one keeps to oneself and would obviously not wish to be made public is probably a private fact. Thus, private debts, criminal records, certain diseases, psychological problems, and the like usually involve private facts.

There is some seemingly private information which courts will treat as public. For purposes of defining potential invasion of privacy liability, "official public records" include legislative, judicial, and executive records and records of documents affecting title to property, such as deeds and vehicle title transfers. Therefore, information contained in a public record is never considered to be private. This principle was firmly established by the Supreme Court in the mid-'70s in *Cox Broadcasting Corp. v. Cohn*. At issue was the constitutionality of a Georgia statute which made it a misdemeanor to publicly disclose the identity of a rape victim. In violation of this statute, someone at the broadcasting company made known the name of a rape victim, based upon information gleaned from a court indictment. The plaintiff, the father of the deceased victim, sued the broadcaster for publicly disclosing private facts, arguing that the statute converted the information into private facts. The highest Georgia court ruled in favor of the father, but when the case reached the Supreme Court, the decision was reversed. In a sweeping opinion, the Court declared that no one could be liable for truthfully disclosing information contained in an official court record, or, by implication, any other public record. Such disclosures enjoy an "absolute privilege" and are treated as public facts, regardless of how personal the information may be. An absolute privilege also exists for public disclosure of private facts made in the context of judicial, legislative, or executive proceedings.

The second requirement a plaintiff must meet in a case for public disclosure is proving that the public disclosure of private facts would be offensive to a reasonable person of ordinary sensibilities. Although a recluse may place a very high premium on absolute privacy, the law does not give such special rights. If a disclosure is minimal and therefore not offensive to the sensibilities of reasonable persons, the recluse will have no cause of action even though, from a recluse's personal perspective, the disclosure may seem egregious.

Disclosures of newsworthy information are generally protected by the First Amendment. As long as such disclosure is truthful, the disclosure is privileged, and an individual's right to privacy will outweigh First Amendment freedoms only when the disclosure is outrageous in the extreme. This privilege regarding newsworthy information significantly insulates media photographers from liability for invasion of privacy.

Photographs with seemingly private subject matter tend to be treated as public if the photographs were taken in public places. For example, in *Alderson v. Fisher Broadcasting Companies, Inc.*, the Oregon Supreme Court refused to recognize an accident victim's claims that his privacy was invaded by a tape shown in an ad for a news feature on emergency medical care. The court held that unless the plaintiff could prove fraud or intentional infliction of emotional distress, there was no liability even though the facts contained on the tape were not newsworthy. Similarly, courts have ruled that neither a photograph of a couple embracing in a marketplace nor a photograph of a defendant in a courtroom were actionable.

Generally, truthful disclosures pertaining to public figures or public officials are considered newsworthy, at least to the extent that the disclosure bears some reasonable relationship to the public role. If, however, the disclosure is highly personal, such as sexual habits, and has no bearing upon the individual's public role, the disclosure may not be privileged and thus may be actionable. This is particularly true where the individual does not enjoy a great deal of fame or notoriety. A presidential candidate or a mass murderer, for example, could expect considerably greater intrusions into and disclosure of his or her private affairs than a minor public official or a one-time traffic offender. Similarly, private individuals who are involuntarily thrust into the public light will receive more protection than those who seek fame and notoriety.

A person no longer in the public eye may or may not be considered newsworthy. Some people, of course, remain newsworthy even though they have long since left the public eye, but generally, the newsworthiness of people who once were public officials or public figures tends to decrease with the passage of time. To the extent that these people become less newsworthy, their right to privacy becomes stronger.

Melvin v. Reid, decided in 1931, illustrates the point. The plaintiff in this case was a former prostitute who had been charged with murder but was acquitted after a rather sensational trial. Thereafter, she led a conventional life; she married and made new friends who were unaware of her sordid past. Some years after the trial, a movie of the woman's early life was made, in which she was identified by her maiden name. She sued, alleging public disclosure of private facts, and the court ruled in her favor. The court conceded that the events that initially brought the woman into the public eye remained newsworthy, but stated that to identify her by name constituted a "willful and wanton disregard of the charity which should actuate us in our social intercourse." The moviemakers' disclosure was deemed so outrageous that it could not be considered newsworthy and the disclosure privilege therefore did not apply.

The case of *Briscoe v. Reader's Digest Association, Inc.* provides an interesting contrast. In this 1971 case, the *Reader's Digest* had published an article about truck hijacking. The article related a hijack attempt involving the plaintiff, Briscoe, who was identified by name. During the years between the hijack attempt and the defendant's disclosure, Briscoe had led an exemplary life. He sued for public disclosure of private facts, alleging that as a result of the article he had been shunned and abandoned by his daughter and friends, who previously had not known of the incident.

Although the facts of *Briscoe* were very similar to those of *Melvin*, and although the issue of outrageous disclosure was raised, the information in the *Briscoe* case was considered newsworthy and thus privileged. That this disclosure was considered newsworthy, whereas the disclosure in the *Melvin* case was not, might best be explained by the fact that the *Melvin* disclosure intruded upon the sex life of the plaintiff, revealing that she had once been a prostitute. It would appear that a disclosure is most likely to be considered unconscionable, and thus not newsworthy, if it relates to someone's sexuality, which is perhaps the most private aspect of anyone's life.

It should be observed that the *social mores* or *outrageous disclosure* test applies only where the plaintiff is in some way newsworthy. A public disclosure involving an ordinary person who is not newsworthy will be actionable if it is merely offensive to the sensibilities of reasonable persons. So, the question is really one of degree.

One final question that has been the subject of litigation in this area is whether an excerpt taken from a publication and used in an advertisement is privileged to the same extent as it is in the original publication. Although the answer is not altogether clear, it appears to depend on whether the advertisement is used to promote the work from which the excerpt was taken or to promote something else.

In *Friedan v. Friedan*, the defendant, Betty Friedan, the noted feminist, wrote and published an account of her early domestic life. She included several photographs of those early years, one of which was a family portrait of her, her former husband, and their child. This picture was selected for use in a television commercial promoting the defendant's publication. Carl Friedan, the defendant's former husband, sued her, alleging that the original publication, as well as the advertisements, constituted an invasion of his privacy as a public disclosure of private facts.

The court easily disposed of Carl Friedan's case. Since Betty Friedan was a noted feminist, her life was a matter of public interest. By virtue of being her former spouse, Carl Friedan also became newsworthy, despite the fact that he had persistently sought to avoid publicity. Because he was deemed newsworthy, the public disclosure about his past private life was permissible. As to the commercial, the court held that where an advertisement is used to promote the publication from which the excerpt was taken, the advertisement will enjoy the same protection as the original publication. Since Betty Friedan's biographical account was permissible, the television commercial was also permissible.

The case of *Rinaldi v. Village Voice, Inc.* involved a slightly different situation. The plaintiff was a prominent judge. *The Village Voice* published an article critical of his performance on the bench. There was no question as to whether the article was permissible, since the plaintiff was clearly newsworthy and the disclosure pertained to his public role. At issue was the question of whether *The Village Voice* could incorporate excerpts from that article into an advertisement for itself. The court held that the advertisement was not permissible since the excerpts were used for the purpose of increasing subscriptions for subsequent issues of the newspaper. *The Village Voice* was held liable for public disclosure of private facts. Had the advertisement been used to promote the particular issue from which the excerpts were taken, it would, presumably, have been permissible under the reasoning applied in *Friedan*.

Where excerpts or photographs are used for purposes other than advertising, such as the circulation of galley proofs of forthcoming books to newspapers and magazines for review, the excerpts or photographs are more likely to enjoy the same privilege as information published in complete form. In *Estate of Hemingway v. Random House, Inc.*, Ernest Hemingway's widow brought an action against the writer and publisher of the book *Papa Hemingway*. The author had drawn largely on his own recollections of conversations with Ernest Hemingway, and included two chapters on the famous novelist's illness and death. The court found that Hemingway was clearly a public figure and rejected the widow's argument that the description of her feelings and conduct during the time of her husband's mental illness was so intimate and unwarranted as to constitute outrageous disclosure. The court also rejected her claim that even if disclosures in the book were protected by the First Amendment, circulation of galley proofs to book reviewers of sixteen journals and newspapers amounted to unlawful use of private facts for advertising purposes. In holding that circulation of proofs to reviewers is not generally advertisement, the court stated:

> A publisher, in circulating a book for review, risks unfavorable comment as well as praise; he places the work in the arena of debate. The same reasons which support the author's freedom to write and publish books require a similar freedom for their circulation, before publication, for comment by reviewers.

In summary, a public disclosure of private facts will support a lawsuit if the effect of the disclosure would be objectionable to persons of ordinary sensibilities, unless the disclosure is newsworthy. Whether a disclosure is or is not newsworthy will depend upon the social value of the facts disclosed, the extent to which the plaintiff voluntarily assumed public fame or notoriety, and the extent to which the disclosure related to the plaintiff's public role. Finally, even a disclosure relating to newsworthy persons may be actionable if it would outrage reasonable persons.

Portrayal of Another in a False Light

Portrayal of another in a false light has been actionable as an invasion of privacy for some time. In 1816, in what was probably the first case to address the issue, the poet Lord Byron successfully enjoined the publication under his name of a rather bad poem which he did not in fact write. Byron was extremely protective of his reputation and apparently felt that the inferior piece would harm his image as an artist.

To bring a suit for false light, a plaintiff must prove that the defendant publicly portrayed the plaintiff in a false light and that the portrayal would be offensive to reasonable people had the damage been done to them. In cases involving the media, the plaintiff must also prove that the portrayal was done with malice.

Thus, false-light cases often involve works that falsely ascribe to the plaintiff particular conduct or action. Usually, photographs do not portray their subjects in a false light, but the accompanying caption or story may, in conjunction with the photograph, create a false impression. For instance, a caption which suggested that two nude models who were photographed together were lesbians was found to be a false-light invasion of privacy in *Douglass v. Hustler Magazine, Inc.*

Leverton v. Curtis Publishing Co. is another example. A young girl who had been struck by an automobile was photographed while a bystander lifted her to her feet, and that photograph appeared in a local newspaper the following day. Nearly two years later the *Saturday Evening Post* published an article entitled "They Ask to Be Killed," the gist of which was that most pedestrian injuries are the result of carelessness on the part of the pedestrian. The photograph of the girl was used to illustrate the story. The girl sued the *Post* for invasion of privacy, alleging among other things that the Post had portrayed her in a false light. The court ruled in her favor because the rational inference from the use of the photograph in the article was that the plaintiff had been injured because of her carelessness, when in fact she had been completely without fault. Thus, the *Post*'s portrayal of the accident victim as having engaged in careless conduct was essentially false.

A frequent cause of false-light cases involves publications that attribute to someone views or opinions that the person does not actually hold or statements that the person did not make.

An extreme case is *Spahn v. Julian Messner, Inc.* in which the defendant published a biography of Warren Spahn, a renowned baseball player. This biography was replete with fictionalized events, dramatizations, distorted chronologies, and fictionalized dialogues. Although the biography tended to glorify Spahn, it nevertheless placed him in a false, albeit radiant, light. As a result, the publisher was held liable for invasion of privacy.

Between the extreme in *Spahn* and a situation where the errors are irrelevant and minimal, it is difficult to predict where liability will lie. Distortions or inaccuracies involving insignificant events, places, and dates are likely to be safe, provided the errors are not pervasive. However, false statements pertaining to significant aspects of someone's life are more likely to result in liability, particularly if they involve highly personal and sensitive matters. The crucial question is whether the false portrayal would be offensive to a reasonable person in the position of the person portrayed. Was the plaintiff, as a result of the publication, humiliated, estranged from friends or family, or embarrassed?

False Light and Defamation: Similarities and Differences

In addition to proving an objectionable portrayal in a false-light case, the plaintiff might also have to prove malice — as is necessary in defamation. Defamation and false-light invasion of privacy have much in common, so that as the law evolves with respect to one, the other is also affected. In 1964, the Supreme Court in *New York Times Co. v. Sullivan* articulated a new requirement for liability in defamation cases: Where the plaintiff is a public figure, public official, or otherwise newsworthy, and where the defendant is a member of the media, the plaintiff must prove that the allegedly defamatory statement was made with malice. Malice is shown if the defendant knew the statement was false or published the statement with reckless disregard for its truth or falsity. The Court felt that an unreasonable limitation on First Amendment freedoms would result if liability was imposed for mere negligence or failure to use due care in ascertaining truth or falsity.

The *New York Times* rule was at first limited to defamation cases. It thus was fairly easy for a newsworthy plaintiff to avoid the more stringent proof-of-malice requirement by couching the complaint in terms of invasion of privacy rather than defamation. If a suit for invasion of privacy could be maintained, the plaintiff could prevail over the media defendant by simply proving negligence.

This rather obvious means of circumventing the *New York Times* rule was done away with three years later in *Time, Inc v. Hill*. The Supreme Court took the opportunity to extend the rationale of *New York Times* to false-light cases of invasion of privacy. A few years earlier, a family named Hill had been held hostage by escaped convicts, and the incident was subsequently portrayed in a play which differed in many material respects from the actual incident. After the play was written, *Life* magazine published a story on the incident which identified the Hills by name and stated as fact some of the fictionalized and dramatized parts of the play. In the Hills' suit, the Court required proof of malice even though the action was for invasion of privacy rather than defamation. As a result, newsworthy plaintiffs suing media defendants either for defamation or for invasion of privacy based upon public portrayal in a false light must prove that the defendant published with malice.

Although defamation and false-light cases are substantially similar, they do differ in three respects. First, the nature of the injury is different. Defamation is injury to the plaintiff's reputation within the community. False light is more inclusive, extending to injuries to the plaintiff's sensibilities caused by personal embarrassment, humiliation, estrangement of loved ones, and the like. Second, truth is an absolute defense for defamation, whereas it may not be for a false-light claim. This is because statements that might in fact be true or photographs that might be accurate may be published out of context so that the plaintiff is nevertheless presented in a false light. Finally, in defamation cases where the plaintiff is a private person who, by circumstances beyond his or her control, is thrust into the public eye, media defendants will be held liable for mere negligence, rather than malice. But in false-light cases, all newsworthy plaintiffs, whether or not they have voluntarily assumed their public role, must prove malice on the part of a media defendant.

Commercial Appropriation of Another's Name or Likeness

Commercial appropriation of someone's name or likeness as an invasion of privacy bears little resemblance to cases based upon wrongful intrusion, public disclosure of private facts, or portrayal in a false light. In all of those situations, the plaintiff must prove that the defendant's words or pictures caused the plaintiff to suffer humiliation, embarrassment, or loss of self-esteem, focusing on the injury to the plaintiff's sensibilities. In contrast, the law against appropriation is designed to protect someone's privately-owned or commercial interest in one's own name or likeness. Athletes, movie stars, authors, and other celebrities obviously receive a considerable amount of their income from the controlled exploitation of their names or likenesses. The monetary benefits from such exploitation would be minimal without some legal protection.

In order to bring a suit for this type of invasion of privacy, one need only prove that the defendant wrongfully appropriated the plaintiff's name or likeness for commercial purposes. "Appropriation" in this sense means use. The fact of appropriation is rarely at issue in these cases, since the use will be obvious. However, the purpose of the use must be commercial, or expected to bring profits, either directly or indirectly. A purely private use will not result in liability for wrongful appropriation.

As with the other kinds of invasion of privacy, any use that is considered newsworthy or informative will not be actionable as a commercial appropriation, even though some commercial gain might result from the use. As you might suspect, whether a use is newsworthy or informative is often difficult to determine.

Namath v. Sports Illustrated involved the use of a celebrity's likeness in an advertisement. *Sports Illustrated* published an article about the 1969 Super Bowl game that included some photographs of Joe Namath. One of those photographs was subsequently used in an advertisement promoting the magazine. Namath sued, alleging that the use of his photograph was a wrongful commercial appropriation. The court held for the magazine, maintaining that its use of Namath's picture was primarily informative because it indicated the general content and nature of the magazine as well as what subscribers could expect to receive in the future. Commercial benefits were only incidental. However, if *Sports Illustrated* had used Namath's picture in such a way that it appeared that Namath endorsed the magazine, the use would have been actionable, since the commercial purpose could not be said to be incidental to the dissemination of information.

In *Booth v. Curtis Publishing Co.*, *Holiday* magazine shot and published a photograph of actress Shirley Booth as part of a news story about a resort. Miss Booth consented to this use of her photograph but brought suit when *Holiday* republished her photograph six months later as part of an advertisement for *Holiday* subscriptions. Here, too, the court denied relief, holding that *Holiday*'s use of the photograph fell within the special exemption for incidental advertising of a news medium itself. The court also noted that the actress was properly and fairly presented. The court reasoned that the magazine used the photographs solely to illustrate the quality and content of the magazine and that, therefore, the use of the photographs was incidental.

Clearly, use of someone's name or likeness in solicitation or advertisement may not be actionable if the use is newsworthy or if the advertising is incidental to informational purposes.

A commercial misappropriation, as well as false-light invasion of privacy, was found in *Douglass v. Hustler Magazine, Inc.*, which concerned photographs published in *Hustler*. The pictures had been taken with the model's consent, but she understood that they would appear in *Playboy*. The court found that model-actress Robin Douglass's right to publicize herself was undermined when *Hustler* deprived her of the choice of publications in which her pictures would appear. However, the court found that *Hustler*'s publication of stills from a movie in which Douglass appeared was not misappropriation because the still photographs were in the public domain and, therefore, beyond Douglass's control.

In suing for unauthorized commercial appropriation, a person is exercising the *right of publicity*, which is defined as a person's right to exploit his or her name, likeness, or reputation and is commonly applied to entertainers and other famous people. In a fairly recent case, the right of publicity was held to be limited by certain aspects of the federal copyright law. In *Baltimore Orioles v. Major League Baseball Players*, baseball players sued club owners, asserting that their performances during ball games were being telecast without the players' consent and that under state law, the telecasting constituted a misappropriation of the players' property right of publicity in their performances. The court found that the players' performance was within the scope of their employment and thus the club owners owned the copyright to the performance. When state and federal law conflict, the federal law takes precedence. In this case, the players' rights of publicity in the game-time performances, as granted by state law, were found to be preempted by federal copyright law.

Appropriation after a Celebrity's Death

A final question is whether a lawsuit based upon commercial appropriation can be brought after the death of the person whose name or likeness was used. There is considerable controversy over this issue.

In a 1984 case in New York, the court denied the defendants the right to name their theatre after playwright Tennessee Williams without his estate's consent. The court held that New York recognizes a common-law right of publicity, and ruled that the right of publicity survives death and descends to the deceased's heirs.

In a similar case involving the Elvis Presley estate, the plaintiff, Factors Etc., Inc., had acquired the exclusive right to market the name and likeness of Elvis Presley during Presley's lifetime. The issue was whether the license remained effective after Presley's death.

Factors Etc. sued, after Presley's death, to prevent another company from distributing posters bearing Presley's image. The federal court, sitting in New York and applying New York law, ruled in favor of Factors, holding that when a party has the right to exploit a name or likeness during the lifetime of the subject, the right survives that person's death.

In another case involving the same license and essentially the same facts, but decided in the state of Tennessee under Tennessee law, the court reached the opposite opinion. The Memphis Development Foundation had solicited money from the public for purposes of erecting a statue of Presley. A donation of twenty-five dollars or more entitled the contributor to an eight-inch pewter replica of the statue. The foundation sought a court ruling on whether the exclusive license of Factors Etc., Inc. to Presley's likeness was still valid. This time the court held that a suit based upon commercial appropriation will under no circumstances survive the death of the person portrayed.

Since then the Tennessee legislature has passed a statute which explicitly states that the right to publicity will survive death and pass to the heir of the person whose name or likeness is commercially appropriated. Several other states, including California, Florida, Oklahoma, and Virginia, have passed similar laws. Such statutes guarantee the survival of such a right regardless of whether the person's name was commercially exploited during life. However, some states, while recognizing that the right to publicity can survive death, maintain that it will do so only if it was commercially exploited during life.

This raises a difficult question because it gives no rights to the heirs of those famous individuals who chose not to exploit their names and faces while alive. Nevertheless, in *Martin Luther King Jr. Center For Social Change, Inc. v. American Heritage*, Coretta Scott King persuaded the court to enjoin American Heritage from selling plastic busts of Dr. King even though Dr. King had not commercially exploited his fame during life.

Since the law is unsettled on whether the right to sue for commercial appropriation survives death, it is difficult to make a general statement about the scope of such a right. Perhaps the most that can be said currently is that more and more courts and legislatures are recognizing that death should not automatically extinguish a right as meaningful and valuable as the right to control the use of a person's name or likeness. Many legal commentators approve this trend.

Photographs of Buildings, Sites, or Objects

Photographers should be aware that owners of buildings, locations or objects may have a protected interest in exploiting images of those properties. The exclusive right to exploit the likenesses of one's build-ings, land or other possessions is technically a property right, rather than a right of privacy, but the legal repercussions of photographing a building may be equivalent to the legal consequences of photographing a person. In *New York World's Fair 1964-65 Corp. v. Colourpicture Pub. Inc.*, the court held that the defendant's photograph of a unique building had invaded a property right of the plaintiff when the photographer commercially exploited the photograph.

Releases

Use of a photograph without written consent always raises the possibility of a lawsuit based on violation of some aspect of right to privacy. The surest and simplest way to avoid right-to-privacy suits is to obtain a release from the subject of the picture, or a release from the owner of any property photographed. (See Chapter 12)

In some states, such as New York, a photographer must obtain written consent for the use of a person's photograph in advertising or promotion. Although an oral release may be legally valid, it may also be difficult to enforce. Therefore, a release should be in writing.

Generally, contracts require consideration—something that indicates compensation for a service rendered. As a release might be considered a contract, it is probably wise to pay the subject at least a small amount. However, one authority has stated that photographic releases are valid even when the photographer pays the subject nothing in modeling fees or use rights.

Most form releases are designed to protect the photographer. However, if a model has been hired by an advertising agency, the release should also cover the agency and the agency's client. A release should be drafted to include permission for the photographer to take the picture and permission for the photographer to make a certain use of the picture.

It is common for a photographer to use a standard release form; however, this form should be used intelligently and modified as needed. Each release should specifically, if briefly, describe the subject matter and the use the photographer plans to make of the picture. A photographer would be wise to stamp the photograph with the same date as the date on the release form; this prevents any confusion or ambiguity as to what is covered when the photograph is released.

The protection of a release is no greater than the use the subject intends to grant. In *Buller v. Pulitzer*

Pub. Co., the court pointed out that, while a valid release waives the subject's right to sue for invasion of privacy, the burden of proof is upon the photographer to show just what was consented to. In *Russell v. Marboro Books*, a fashion model posed reading in bed, fully clothed, for an advertisement to promote a book club. The model signed a broadly-worded waiver that allowed the book club to make unrestricted use of the photograph. However, when the book company sold the photograph to a bed sheet manufacturer who retouched the photo, putting the title of a well-known pornographic book on the book the model held in the picture and running the photo with sexually suggestive copy, the model sued, alleging that her personal and professional standing were damaged by the bed sheet ad. The court awarded her damages based on invasion of privacy and libel, reasoning that the release was ineffective because the content of the photograph was altered so as to make it substantially unlike the original. Thus, a release should include a clause granting the right to alter a photograph and granting the right to add any type of copy or captions.

In the event a photographer has not obtained a release on a particular photograph, he may achieve limited protection against a third party's unauthorized use of the photograph by stating on the back of the picture: "This photograph cannot be altered for commercial or advertising use nor can it be copied, televised or reproduced in any form without the photogapher's permission."

Photographers should be aware that a release signed by the parent of a child subject may not in all instances be valid. Current court decisions uphold the validity of releases signed by parents; however, language in these cases indicates that courts would refuse to find the releases binding in certain circumstances.

In *Faloona v. Hustler Magazine, Inc.*, the mother of two minor children executed a full release to a photographer for the use of nude photographs of her children. The children and their mother sued the photographer when the children's picture appeared in *Hustler* magazine. While not objecting to the photographs, per se, the plaintiffs believed that publication in *Hustler* constituted false-light invasion of privacy, public disclosure of private facts, and commercial misappropriation. The court applied Texas law, which provides that a parent has the authority to consent to matters of substantial legal significance concerning a child, and dismissed the case. New York and California have laws similar to those of Texas on the issue of

parental consent; presumably, similar cases would have the same outcome in these jurisdictions. However, in *Faloona*, *Hustler* showed the children's photo to illustrate a review of a sex education book in which the photo originally appeared. Had Hustler used the photo in a salacious manner, the court probably would have invalidated the consent.

In *Shields v. Gross*, the court held that when the parent or guardian of a minor gives unrestricted consent to a photographer to make a commercial use of the minor's photograph, the minor may not later on make use of the common-law right to break a contract entered into while she was a minor. However, photographers should be aware that this case contains a strong dissent and the holding was influenced by the fact Ms. Shields was a professional actress, although a child. The holding has evoked critical commentary, as many believe that a minor's right to privacy should supersede the business community's interest in binding minors to contractual terms. The law may change in the future to reflect this philosophy.

Some states, one of which is California, have legislation *requiring* photographers to obtain a permit before using a minor as a model. These laws, known as Jackie Coogan legislation, impose complicated and expensive requirements on photographers who photograph minors. Therefore, it is advisable to check with a local attorney before you use a child model.

The Photographer's Right of Access

As important as the photographic subject's right to privacy is the photographer's right to take pictures. Neither of these rights is absolute; rather, the subject's right of privacy and the photographer's right to take pictures are the mirror image of one another and one right ends where the other begins.

Generally, photographers have a right to take pictures so long as they do not invade their subjects' privacy or make a public nuisance of themselves. Ordinarily, you can take pictures in concert halls, theaters, museums, hospitals and nursing homes so long as you do not infringe copyrights by doing so and so long as the institution in question has no clear rules or regulations to the contrary. If an institution has a clearly posted prohibition against taking photographs, you may be liable for trespass if you proceed to take pictures. In addition, there are some statutes which prohibit photographing certain buildings or sites such as the federal prohibition against photographing post offices or military installations. The federal government also prohibits the commercial exploitation of photographs of federal land without express permission.

Photojournalists tend to have somewhat more legal protection of their right of access to subjects if those subjects are newsworthy. The United States Supreme Court has recognized that the First Amendment protects the media's right to publish news. However, news media have no constitutional right of access to the scenes of crime or disaster when the general public is excluded. Basically, the United States Supreme Court has held that as long as restrictions treat the media and the public equally, they are constitutional. However, some recent cases indicate that news professionals may have more rights than the general public.

Newsworthy events often occur in public places such as streets, sidewalks or parks. These places are public forums because they are open to the public and few restrictions are placed on the activities which may take place in them. Reporters can be barred from covering activities in public forums only if news-gathering restrictions are reasonable.

In New York City, there are several sections of the administrative code that require permits in order to take motion pictures or to telecast or to photograph in public places. Other sections of New York City's code forbid the use of tripods in public parks.

Not all property owned by the government is considered a public forum. Federal courthouses, jails, government offices and city halls are not usually open for general public use. Therefore, in many cases courts have not allowed the media access to such property.

When municipal property is not operated by the municipality, the media have only the same right of access as the general public.

Many newsworthy events occur on private property. Property owners may restrict access to their homes, businesses, shopping centers and privately owned housing developments. Even when property owners have not barred access, they have been able to obtain damages for trespass or invasion of privacy when they did not consent to the journalist's entry. A key issue in such cases is whether the owner's silence was the effective equivalent of consent. In a Florida case, an invasion-of-privacy suit was brought against a newspaper for publishing a photograph of the silhouette of the body of a seventeen-year-old girl killed in a house fire. The fire marshal and a police sergeant investigating the fire invited the news media into the burned-out home to cover the story. In court,

they testified that their invitation was standard practice. The property owner, who was the victim's mother, was out of town at the time of the fire. Therefore, she was not present to be asked for permission. Clearly, the fire was of great public interest because of the damage done to the house, because a person had died, and because arson was suspected. The court found implied consent and ruled in favor of the media, with the qualification that if the owner had been present and objected to the reporter's presence, the reporter might have been liable for damages.

Photojournalists should be aware that state constitutions may provide greater protection for the media than does the United States Constitution. In California, the state constitution guarantees access to news on private business property.

However, if the police order you not to enter an area in pursuit of news, you are risking arrest, prosecution and liability by disregarding the order, whether or not the property in question is public or privately owned. In *Stahl v. Oklahoma*, several reporters were arrested for following anti-nuclear power demonstrators onto a privately-owned power-plant site. The owner of the land, the Public Service Co. of Oklahoma, had denied both the public and the media access to the plant. The court treated the plant as a government entity because the power company's activities were heavily regulated by the state and federal government. Nonetheless, the judge fined the reporters for criminal trespass, ruling that the First Amendment does not guarantee access to property simply because it is owned or controlled by the government nor does the First Amendment protect reporters from arrest and prosecution if they have broken the law while gathering news.

Police departments across the country are under pressure to develop guidelines governing their relationship with the media. If a police department provides guidelines governing access to crime scenes and issues press credentials, the guidelines must not result in the arbitrary denial of access to certain journalists. In *Sherrill v. Knight*, the court held that if an agency establishes a policy of admitting the media, even though the public is barred, media access cannot later be denied arbitrarily or for less than compelling reasons. It also ruled that agencies must publish the standards that will be used in deciding whether an applicant is eligible to receive a press pass and that journalists who are denied press passes must be provided with reasons for the denial and given an opportunity to appeal.

Since the legal concepts discussed in this chapter are still evolving, and since their treatment varies from state to state, you as a photographer would be well advised to work closely with a lawyer when a question arises regarding invasion of a right to privacy.

Chapter 4

CENSORSHIP AND OBSCENITY

The First Amendment of the United States Constitution states in part, "Congress shall make no law ... abridging the freedom of speech, or of the press." First Amendment absolutists insist that the words are all-encompassing and that no law should ever be enacted that places any restriction whatsoever on the free exercise of speech or press. Although a strict reading of the Constitution may support this opinion, the judiciary has never fully upheld it and has ruled that certain types of speech are not protected by the First Amendment.

Two theories have been used to justify exceptions to First Amendment protection. The first theory maintains that although certain expressions do normally deserve First Amendment protection, such protection will not be forthcoming if another right, either public or private, outweighs the citizen's First Amendment rights. Examples of speech (which has been defined as including photographs) that are not absolutely protected include defamatory remarks, remarks that advocate unlawful conduct, and remarks that invade someone's privacy. The second theory suggests that certain expressions do not constitute speech for purposes of First Amendment protection because they are without serious social value. Under this theory, courts often maintain that obscene works are not protected.

Prior Restraint

When the First Amendment was being written, the memory of the English licensing system, under which nothing could be published without prior approval, was still vivid in the minds of the framers of the Constitution. Some historians suggest that the First Amendment was written specifically to prevent such prior restraints. Today the First Amendment means more than freedom from prepublication censorship, but because of its potential for abuse, censorship before publication is still considered more serious than restrictions imposed after publication. The Supreme Court in *Near v. Minnesota* recognized that "liberty of the press ... has meant, principally although not exclusively, immunity from previous restraints and censorship."

Prior restraints impose an extreme burden upon the exercise of free speech since they limit open debate and the unfettered dissemination of knowledge. It is not surprising that the Supreme Court has almost universally found that it is unconstitutional to restrain speech prior to a determination of whether the speech is protected by the First Amendment.

Prohibition of Political Speech

A prior-restraint lawsuit generally begins with a request, often by the government, for a court order prohibiting publication of information already in the media's possession. Where controversial political speech is involved, the government may argue that publication will cause substantial and irreparable harm to the United States. In *New York Times Co. v. United States*, for example, the government tried to stop the publication of the Pentagon Papers, which detailed U.S. involvement in Vietnam prior to 1968. The government claimed that publication would prolong the war and embarrass the United States in the conduct of its diplomacy.

The Supreme Court found that the government's claim of potential injury to the U.S. was insufficient to justify prior restraint. The justices, although believing that publication would probably be harmful, were not persuaded that publication would "surely" cause the harm alleged. Justice Potter Stewart agreed and wrote a concurring opinion emphasizing that the government must show that disclosure "will surely result in direct, immediate, and irreparable damage to our nation or its people."

In a later case, *United States v. The Progressive, Inc.*, the government used a similar argument: national security. In the *Progressive* case, the government sought to prohibit publication of a magazine article which detailed a method for constructing a hydrogen bomb. The government's case was weak for a variety of reasons, not the least of which was the fact that the alleged secrets were not then classified and had in fact been published in books, journals, magazines, and the government's own reports. Any diligent reporter could have uncovered the same information. Perhaps realizing the impossibility of meeting the test of "direct, immediate, irreversible harm" laid out in the 1971 Pentagon Papers case, the government abandoned the suit, but not until after raising the chilling threat of prior restraint.

Prohibition of Pretrial Publicity

Another kind of suppression of the free flow of information involves the restriction of pretrial publicity. Here the conflict is between the individual's right to a fair trial and the right of the press to its First Amendment guarantee of free speech. This conflict was addressed in *Nebraska Press Association v. Stuart.*

The Nebraska Press Association appealed a court order prohibiting the press from reporting on confessions and other information implicating an accused murderer after the murder of six family members had gained widespread public attention. The trial judge originally issued the order because he felt that pretrial publicity would make it difficult to select a jury that had not been exposed to prejudicial press coverage.

The Supreme Court nonetheless struck down the trial judge's order, finding that the impact of publicity on jurors was "speculative, dealing with factors unknown and unknowable." The justices went on to suggest alternatives to restraining all publication, including changing the location of the trial, postponing the trial, asking in-depth questions of prospective jury members during the selection process to determine bias, explicitly instructing the jury to consider only evidence presented at trial, and isolating the jury.

This decision appears to go far in requiring that other methods of pretrial precautions be taken, and that an order restricting press coverage be used only as a last resort. While this case involved press coverage, the same rule should apply to a photographer who wishes to publish a photograph of the scene of a crime or one which may be involved in litigation.

Prohibition of Commercial Speech

In other areas, however, the Court has been more tolerant of prior restraints. For example, the Court held in *Virginia State Board of Pharmacy v. Virginia Consumer Council* that prior restraints are sometimes permissible when purely commercial speech such as advertisements or other promotional material is involved. In that case the Court considered the constitutionality of a Virginia statute which prohibited pharmacists from advertising prices of prescription drugs. The Court held that the statute was unconstitutional and thereby rejected the notion that commercial speech is never entitled to First Amendment protection. However, the Court distinguished commercial speech from ordinary speech in discussing the application of the First Amendment to it. The Court reasoned that since commercial statements are generally objective in content, whether they are true or false can be readily determined. Thus, the Court believed that there was little or no threat of prior restraints being arbitrarily imposed. In addition, the Court maintained that commercial speech lacks the urgency which often accompanies noncommercial speech, so that any delay caused by the restraint while its justification is being argued would be relatively harmless. Since many of the dangers associated with prior restraints (such as suppression of political dissent) were not deemed to be present, the Court ruled that prior restraints of commercial speech are not always unconstitutional. Here, too, the rule announced by the court should apply to prior restraint imposed on photographs.

Prohibition of Obscene Speech

Prior restraints have also been upheld where the suppressed material was obscene, but the Supreme Court has imposed several procedural safeguards for this type of case. For example: (1) the accused must be given a prompt hearing; (2) the government agency making the accusation carries the burden of showing that the material is, in fact, obscene; (3) a valid final restraint can be issued only after a judicial proceeding; and (4) once the government agency has itself made a finding of obscenity, it must take action on its own behalf in a court of law to confirm its own finding.

Prior restraints on commercial speech and alleged obscenity are less often condemned by the courts because the immediately topical nature of and public interest in the free flow of "political speech" are not characteristic of commercial or sexual expressions; therefore, the public interest is not compromised as much by delays in publication of sexual expressions. As Justice John Harlan commented in *A Quantity of Books v. Kansas,* "sex is of constant but rarely particularly topical interest."

The Scope of Permissible Prior Restraints

It should be emphasized that the major presumption the Court made in *Near v. Minnesota* is still applicable; the chief purpose of the First Amendment's freedom of the press provision was to prevent prior restraints on publication. In *Near*, the Court listed only three situations which "might" justify prior restraint: (1) the need to prevent obstruction of a government's recruiting service, or to prevent publication of the sailing dates of transport ships or the number and location of troops; (2) failure to meet the requirements of decency, as in an obscene publication; and (3) the necessity of avoiding incitement to acts of violence and the overthrow by force of orderly government. These three exceptions, along with the requirements that the government prove with certainty that particular speech is unprotected and is likely to cause irreparable harm, limit the scope of permissible prior restraint.

It is worth noting that the Supreme Court has held that a school could suspend a student because of a speech he made containing numerous sexual metaphors, despite the student's claim of First Amendment protection. The Court felt that the school's right to maintain an appropriate educational environment for children outweighed the student's right of free speech.

Obscenity

Obscenity is perhaps the area where most of the censorship in this country has occurred.

A variety of laws are involved in regulating "obscene materials." Some state laws prohibit publication, distribution, public display or sales to minors of obscene material. Some city ordinances prohibit any commercial dealings in pornography whatsoever. Transporting obscene material across a state line or national border is forbidden by federal law, and it is a crime punishable by up to five years in jail to send obscene materials through the U.S. mail.

Since the private possession of obscene material is not unlawful, one who simply photographs material which could be categorized as obscene has not thereby violated obscenity laws. Of course, if the photographer himself publishes or distributes the material, liability can result. Otherwise, it is the magazine or book publisher who is at risk of violating the law. However, a photographer whose works involve especially graphic sexual scenes may be prevented from publishing or distributing those works because

a court has previously declared the work to be obscene. In addition, the photographer whose work is declared obscene may face a lawsuit from his or her publisher, since many photographer-publisher contracts contain a warranty or indemnity clause stating that nothing in the work is obscene. In the event that the photograph is declared obscene, such a clause entitles the publisher to either sue the photographer directly for breach of warranty, or bill the photographer for any losses the publisher might have incurred in an obscenity suit.

Defining Obscenity

It has been the task of the Supreme Court, as the ultimate interpreter of the Constitution, to devise a definition of obscenity that is specific and at the same time flexible. It must be specific if it is to provide useful guidance to photographers and publishers, and it must be flexible to accommodate changes in social mores and ethics.

As the Court has attempted to formulate a definition which accomplishes these two objectives, the law of obscenity has undergone rapid changes.

The Roth Definition

In *Roth v. United States* a New York publisher and distributor of books, photographs, and magazines was convicted in the 1950s of violating a federal obscenity statute by mailing obscene circulars and advertising an obscene book. He appealed to the U.S. Supreme Court, claiming that his conduct was protected by the First Amendment. The Court rejected this argument and affirmed the conviction, but in the course of its opinion it did away with the standard which had been applied to obscenity cases since 1868, the ancient test devised by a British court in *Regina v. Hicklin*.

The *Regina* court had held that a publication which condemned certain practices of Roman Catholic priests in the confessional was obscene. There, the test for obscenity was "whether the tendency of the matter charged as obscenity is to deprave and corrupt those whose minds are open to such immoral influences and into whose hands a publication of this sort may fall." Because this test dictated that the material be judged according to the effect of an isolated excerpt upon persons of delicate sensibilities, it subjected to threat of censorship any adult treatment of sex, among other things, and endangered the right to publish and distribute many highly acclaimed literary works. In recognition of these problems the Court, in considering *Roth*, set forth a new standard: A work would be considered obscene if "to the average person, applying contemporary community standards, the dominant theme of the material taken as a whole appeals to prurient interest."

It was hoped that *Roth* would stabilize the law of obscenity, but confusion remained nonetheless. In *Jacobellis v. Ohio*, the Supreme Court reversed a conviction for violation of an Ohio statute which prohibited the possession and exhibition of obscene films. The Supreme Court held that the lower court had erroneously construed the phrase "contemporary community standards" to mean local rather than national standards. The Court thought that allowing local standards to govern would have the effect of denying some areas of the country access to materials that were acceptable in those areas, simply because publishers and distributors would be reluctant to risk prosecution under the laws of more conservative states where the same materials would be unacceptable. By applying a national standard to the case, the Court maintained that the film was not obscene. The question remains, however, of how to define the national standard. In *Roth*, it seems to have been found in the personal tastes and predilections of the majority of the justices, particularly in light of Justice Stewart's statement on the nature of obscenity: "I know it when I see it."

The Memoirs Definition

When the attorney general of Massachusetts requested a court order declaring the book *Fanny Hill* obscene, the Massachusetts courts ruled in his favor. On appeal, the Supreme Court in *Memoirs v. Massachusetts* reversed the Massachusetts courts, holding that the mere risk that a work might be exploited by advertisers because of its treatment of sexual matters is not sufficient to make it obscene. Instead, the Court held in a plurality opinion that the prosecution must establish three separate elements to prove obscenity:

(a) the dominant theme of the material taken as a whole appeals to a prurient interest in sex; (b) the material is patently offensive because it affronts contemporary community standards relating to the description or representation of sexual matters; and (c) the material is utterly without redeeming social value.

However, even this three-part test has not brought clarity to the law of obscenity. In 1972, six years after the *Memoirs* decision, the Supreme Court was again confronted with a state court's overly broad definition of obscenity. The case was *Kois v. Wisconsin*.

In *Kois*, the Wisconsin state court convicted the publisher of an underground newspaper of two counts of violating a state obscenity statute which prohibited the dissemination of "lewd, obscene, or indecent written matter, pictures, sound recording, or film." The first count was for publication of an article that reported the arrest of one of the newspaper's photographers on a charge of possession of obscene material. Two relatively small pictures, showing a nude couple embracing in a sitting position, accompanied the article. The second count was for distributing a newspaper containing a poem entitled "Sex Poem," which was a frank, play-by-play account of the author's recollection of sexual intercourse.

The Supreme Court reversed the obscenity conviction, finding that, for the first count, the pictures were rationally related to an article that was clearly entitled to First Amendment protection. As for the second count, the poem had "some of the earmarks of an attempt at serious art."

The Miller Definition

The Supreme Court tried again to provide a workable definition in its 1973 *Miller v. California* decision. In this case, Marvin Miller sent five unsolicited brochures to a restaurant. The brochures advertised four books: *Intercourse, Man-Woman, Sex Orgies Illustrated* and *An Illustrated History of Pornography*. Also included was a film entitled *Marital Intercourse*. The brochures contained pictures of men and women in a variety of sexual positions, with their genitals displayed.

In reviewing *Roth* and *Memoirs*, the Court concluded that one thing had been categorically settled: "Obscene material is unprotected by the First Amendment." But because any limitation on an absolute freedom of expression could lead to undesirable and dangerous censorship, it was deemed essential that state obscenity laws be limited in scope and properly applied. These concerns are manifest in the *Miller* obscenity test, which substantially modified the *Roth-Memoirs* test. The *Miller* test is:

(a) whether "the average person, applying contemporary community standards" would find that the work, taken as a whole, appeals to the prurient interest, (b) whether the work depicts or describes in a patently offensive way, sexual conduct specifically defined by the applicable state law, and (c) whether the work, taken as a whole, lacks serious literary, artistic, political, or scientific values.

Thus, the *Roth-Memoirs* requirement that prosecutors prove that the challenged material is "utterly without social value" was replaced by a new standard which merely required the absence of "serious social value." Moreover, the Court upheld the right of a state to apply a local, rather than a national, standard in enforcing its obscenity laws.

The intent of *Miller* was to provide much clearer guidelines for protected speech, both to state legislatures enacting statutes and to prosecutors enforcing that legislation. *Miller* required that state statutes be more specific, so the states attempted to define the *Miller* test for their own communities. However, instead of clarifying the law, the hodgepodge of legislation spurred by *Miller* has only contributed to the vagueness, increased breadth, and chilling effect of obscenity legislation. Inconsistencies in the laws require the photographer to be aware of local statutes and ordinances in each area where distribution of a given photograph is planned.

Defining "Community Standards"

One of the greatest difficulties courts have had in applying the *Miller* test has involved defining "community" for the purposes of ascertaining moral standards. The Supreme Court said in 1974 that *Miller*'s effect "is to permit the juror in an obscenity case to draw on his own knowledge of the community from which he comes in deciding what conclusion an 'average person' would reach in a given case." The Court, however, does not require that the juror be instructed as to how large the relevant community is geographically. Instructions which direct the jury to apply "community standards" without specifying the boundaries of that community are acceptable. In reaffirming the idea that jurors are to draw on their own knowledge, the Court has emphasized that community standards are not to be defined legislatively.

Recently, the United States Supreme Court modified the third prong of the *Miller* test and held that courts applying *Miller* must determine whether a reasonable person, rather than a given community, would find that "the work, taken as a whole, lacks serious literary, artistic, political, or scientific value." Justice Stevens reasoned that, as far as the First Amendment is concerned, the value of a work does not vary from community to community based on the degree of local acceptance it has won.

Defining "Patently Offensive"

The Supreme Court in *Miller* provided some guid-

ance as to the meaning of "patently offensive," indicating that the phrase refers to "hard-core" materials which, among other things, include "patently offensive representations or descriptions of ultimate sexual acts, normal or perverted, actual or simulated," and "patently offensive representations or descriptions of masturbation, excretory functions, and lewd exhibitions of the genitals." These examples indicate that materials less than "patently offensive" may well be entitled to First Amendment protection, and thus serve as a limitation on the states' power to arbitrarily define obscenity.

In *Jenkins v. Georgia*, the Supreme Court applied this standard to the Academy Award-winning film *Carnal Knowledge*. A Georgia court had convicted the defendant after a jury determined that the film was obscene. Although the Court recognized that the issue of obscenity was primarily a question of fact to be determined by the jury, it was not willing to grant the jury unlimited license in making that determination. Because the Court decided that the film was not sufficiently hard-core to be considered patently offensive, it reversed the jury's decision and the resulting conviction.

Defining the "Prurient Interest" of the "Average Person"

According to the ruling in *Miller*, to be judged obscene, a work must appeal to the "prurient interest" of the "average person." *Prurient interest* is an elusive concept, but that did not stop the Supreme Court from attempting to define it in *Roth* as that which "beckons to a shameful, morbid, degrading, unhealthy, or unwholesome interest in sex." Some states have attempted to write their own definition of prurient interest into their obscenity statutes. One such attempt that was challenged as overly broad led to yet another Supreme Court decision on obscenity in *Brockett v. Spokane Arcades, Inc.*

The statute challenged in *Brockett* defined obscene matter as that appealing to the prurient interest, which was further defined as "that which incites lasciviousness or lust." The Supreme Court held that by including lust in its definition of prurient, the statute extended to material which merely stimulated normal sexual responses. Thus, the statute was overly broad and unconstitutional. The Court indicated that material said to appeal to prurient interests is to be judged by its impact on the normal person, not by its effect on those who are easily influenced or unusually sensitive. Thus, a jury is not to consider the effect the material in question would have on children or adolescents under eighteen. These statements by the Court raise the possibility of a defense argument that if a work obviously appeals to a bizarre or deviant sexual appetite, acquittal is required because the "average person" is not affected. A widely recognized exception to the "average person" standard has been established by the Court, however, where it can be shown that a given book, magazine, or film was designed for and distributed to a well-defined deviant group.

The issue of whether material appeals primarily to the prurient interest may be influenced by the manner in which it is advertised. Evidence of an advertising practice known legally as "pandering" may contribute to the likelihood that a work will be declared obscene. Pandering occurs when materials are marketed by emphasizing their sexually provocative nature.

The relevance of pandering was first determined by the Supreme Court in 1966, in *Ginzburg v. U.S.* In *Ginzburg*, the Supreme Court reviewed a conviction under a federal obscenity statute for distribution of several publications containing erotic materials which, because they were of some value to psychiatrists and other professionals, were not in and of themselves obscene. However, since the defendants had portrayed the materials as salacious and lewd in their marketing, and had indiscriminately distributed those works to the general public, the trial court had found the materials to be obscene. The Supreme Court affirmed, stating that evidence of pandering is relevant to the question of obscenity.

The Supreme Court again upheld the relevance of pandering in *Hamling v. United States*. In that case, the Court made it clear that where the obscenity question is a close one, evidence of pandering may be considered. Such evidence is but one factor in determining whether a work is obscene, however, and does not replace the *Miller* test.

Thematic Obscenity

Thematic obscenity refers to obscenity that is more or less the central theme of a work, and thus is relevant to the ideas the work intends to express. Such material is not completely beyond the states' reach if it is in fact obscene. At the same time, the Supreme Court is extremely suspicious of state obscenity statutes that appear to prohibit sexually explicit materials which convey certain ideas, rather than sexually explicit (and patently offensive) materials in and of themselves.

The Supreme Court addressed thematic obscenity in *Kingsley International Pictures Corp. v. Regents of New York University*. In this case, the Court reviewed a New York statute which forbade licenses for the exhibition of motion pictures that portrayed "acts of sexual immorality ... as desirable, acceptable, or as a proper pattern of behavior." Application of the statute had resulted in denial of a license for *Lady Chatterley's Lover*, a film that portrayed an adulterous relationship.

The Court found that the New York statute went beyond regulating the depiction of patently offensive sexual acts and, in effect, prevented the expression of an idea—namely, that an adulterous relationship could under some circumstances be condoned. Since the right to express ideas is expressly protected by the First Amendment, and since the statute denied that right, the statute was deemed unconstitutional.

Another attempt to suppress thematic obscenity was overturned by the Court in 1962 in *Manual Enterprises v. Day*. This time the Court held that a magazine for homosexuals was not obscene. Obscenity, it said, requires proof of two elements: (1) patent offensiveness and (2) appeal to prurient interest. Since pictures in the magazine under attack were found to be no more objectionable than the pictures of female nudes that society tolerates in other magazines, they could not be prohibited simply because they conveyed the idea of homosexuality.

Federal Statutes

Under the anti-pandering law, people who receive any pandering advertisements which those people find erotically arousing or sexually provocative can notify the Postal Service that they wish to receive no further mailings from the sender, following which the Postal Service is required to issue an order directing the sender of such advertisements to refrain from further mailings to those recipients. The U.S. Supreme Court upheld the validity of the anti-pandering law in *Rowan v. United States Post Office Dept.* In that case the Supreme Court said that a "mailer's right to communicate must stop at the mail box of an unreceptive addressee."

The Postal Reorganization Act of 1970 contains a provision that prohibits the mailing of sexually oriented advertisements to any person who has requested that his name be placed on the Postal Service list of persons desiring not to receive sexually oriented advertising. This law is popularly known as the Goldwater Amendment, and was enacted in an effort to prevent the flow of vulgar or pornographic material into the home of anyone not wishing to be subjected to such mail, while preserving the rights of those who want to receive such material through the mail. The notice authorized under the Goldwater Amendment affects all mailers and not just a particular mailer.

A year's subscription to a copy of the list of those who do not wish to receive sexually oriented ads can be obtained from the Postal Service by a deposit of $5,000 and subsequent payment of charges not to exceed $10,000, including the deposit. A sexually oriented advertisement is defined as

> any advertisement that depicts, in actual or simulated form, or explicitly describes, in a predominantly sexual context, human genitalia, any act of natural or unnatural sexual intercourse, any act of sadism or masochism, or any other erotic subject directly related to the foregoing. [However] material otherwise within the definition of this subsection shall be deemed not to constitute a sexually oriented advertisement if it constitutes only a small and insignificant part of the whole of a single catalog, book, periodical or other work the remainder of which is not primarily devoted to sexual matters.

Child Pornography Legislation

Attempts to regulate pornography have also been made by legislators enacting child pornography laws. This legislation is designed to curb sexual abuse of children by making it unlawful to use children in explicit sexual performances or pornographic pictures. The Supreme Court has been relatively supportive of state efforts to outlaw pornography dealing with children. In the 1982 case of *New York v. Ferber*, the Court held that a state may ban the distribution of materials showing children engaged in sexual conduct even though the material is not legally obscene. State child-pornography laws vary widely. The photographer who plans to sell any pictures of children in sexual circumstances would be well advised to consult with a lawyer.

Forfeiture or Closure Legislation

Photographers should be aware that some states have statutes that make it a crime or a pubic nuisance to disseminate or exhibit obscene material. Usually, these statutes allow the authorities to close or even cause the owner to forfeit the use of the property from which the obscene materials were disseminated. Under some of these statutes authorities may enforce closure or forfeiture of premises even though the material disseminated was "lewd" or "indecent" rather than

actually obscene. Some courts have found these statutes to be unconstitutional prior restraints of non-obscene material. However, other courts have upheld forfeiture statutes, reasoning that no closure or forfeiture takes place until there has been a judicial determination of whether the disseminated material was actually obscene.

Informal Censorship

There is the possibility that government funding could be distributed in such a way as to constitute informal censorship. The problem is illustrated by the case of *Advocates for the Arts v. Thompson*. In that case the plaintiff, Granite Publications, was to receive a grant from the New Hampshire Commission on the Arts, which was funded largely by the National Endowment for the Arts. The commission withdrew its pledge of funding upon discovering that a poem previously published by Granite was, in the commission's opinion, obscene. Granite sued, alleging that its First Amendment rights had been violated. The federal court ruled in favor of the arts commission.

Although the Court was not willing to rule that the poem was obscene under the Miller test, neither was it willing to intrude upon the discretion of the arts commission to determine which projects would or would not receive government funds. As long as it could be argued that the commission's selections were based on the issue of artistic or literary merit, the First Amendment was not violated. The Court did intimate that the commission might not have exercised the best judgment with respect to the poem. Nevertheless, the Court refused to place itself in a position of being the final arbiter of questions of literary merit. Moreover, the Court refused to require the commission to draw up narrow standards and guidelines by which artistic merit could be judged, since these qualities are by their very nature subjective.

The Court concluded that refusal of the government to provide funds for the arts will not normally constitute censorship, since such refusal does not prohibit the publication of a given work, although inability to publish may be the practical result. Photographers may therefore find that their work is unacceptable to publishers who are concerned about this informal type of censorship. This is not to say that government funding agencies are completely immune from attack on the basis of constitutional rights. The court in Thompson did suggest that, should an agency develop a "pattern of discrimination impinging upon the basic First Amendment rights to free and full debate on matters of public interest," an argument concerning the photographer's constitutional rights might have merit.

Once a work has received some form of government funding, the withdrawal of the government sponsorship may be a First Amendment violation. Thus in *American Council for the Blind v. The Librarian of Congress* it was held that Congress's refusal to continue funding for the purpose of putting into Braille and recording *Playboy* magazine infringed the constitutional rights of the plaintiff, the American Council for the Blind.

"Censorship" by Film Processors

Courts have upheld the right of a film processor to refuse to process or return film which the processor deemed obscene. Processors have been allowed to retain allegedly obscene film on three theories: first, that return of the film might make the processor liable under a state obscenity statute; second, that the owner has no right to film which constitutes obscene contraband; and, third, existence of an implied or express contract term that the developer is not required to process or return films of obscene subject matter. In *Penthouse Enter., Ltd. v. Eastman Kodak Co.*, the court held that a film processor had the right to decide what it would refuse to process so long as its policies were applied uniformly, and no First Amendment rights were violated since no state action was involved and the film processor did not censor or restrict what the magazine could publish.

Predicting Liability

As I have indicated here, whether or not a photograph is likely to be deemed obscene under the *Miller* test is extremely difficult to predict. Courts have experienced numerous problems in applying the *Miller* test, and there is no indication that these problems are likely to be resolved in the near future.

Perhaps the most significant barrier to predictability in obscenity cases is that obscenity is a factual question to be determined by a jury. Presumably, juries are composed of reasonable persons, but it has long been recognized that reasonable persons may disagree. Consequently it is not particularly surprising that different juries have come up with different results in obscenity cases involving essentially the same facts and issues.

Censorship in the United States is far from a fading issue or a shrinking problem for the photographer. In fact, passage and enforcement of even more restrictive obscenity laws may be on the horizon. This scenario is recommended to the American people in the report of the United States Attorney General's Commission on Pornography released July 9, 1986.

The eleven-member "Meese Commission," appointed in May of 1985 and stacked unabashedly with anti-vice prosecutors and activists, reviewed social research and conducted over 300 hours of emotional hearings which one critic has referred to as a "show trial in which pornography was found guilty."

The commission wrestled unsuccessfully with the problem of defining pornography, and in the end was unable to articulate any category of sexual imagery which it would consider harmless, ultimately overturning the findings of the 1970 report of the President's Commission on Pornography which had concluded there was no evidence that sexually explicit material caused antisocial behavior.

The Meese Commission not only recommended passage of new state obscenity laws, but also endorsed citizen action groups and provided instructions for canvassing local bookstores and for organizing demonstrations, boycotts, and other grass-roots censorship-oriented activities.

How, then, is the photographer to predict whether a particular jury might reasonably find a photograph to be obscene? You probably cannot make this prediction, at least not without the assistance of a lawyer familiar with the relevant decisions. By analyzing the various obscenity cases in which the defendant was convicted and contrasting them with those in which the defendant was acquitted, and by staying on top of any new obscenity laws which may be enacted in the future, an attorney should be able to provide a fairly accurate prediction as to whether the work in question will or will not be considered obscene. Unfortunately, graphic material such as pictures and films is much more often found to be obscene than written material.

Other Censorship Problems

Censorship of obscene material is only one limitation the government places on photographers' First Amendment rights. In addition, the government forbids the photographing of uncancelled postage stamps, color photographs of money, or the photographing of U.S. military installations that contain secret equipment or facilities.

Also, the federal government and most of the states have enacted flag-desecration statutes that impose civil or criminal liability on persons who deface or mutilate a flag. These statutes were enacted in response to the flag burnings by protestors against the Vietnam War and against civil rights abuses. Generally, flag-desecration statutes are designed to prevent breaches of the peace which might result from improper use of and disrespect to the flag. Thus, *People v. Von Rosen* held that magazine publication of photographs of a nude girl covered by an American flag, though disrespectful, did not violate a state flag-desecration statute because the photographs were not likely to bring about a breach of the peace. However, some courts have recognized other purposes to be served by flag-desecration statutes. In *People v. Keough*, the court found that publication of photographs of a female clothed only in an American flag and a pair of boots, posing with a soldier, was sufficient to be a violation of a state flag-desecration statute because the photographs cast contempt upon the American flag.

Many flag-desecration statutes require that the disrespectful display of the flag be a public one. Under these statutes, a photographer could not be liable for any disrespectful flag photograph until it was published.

In the District of Columbia, it is an offense to use the United States flag or any representation thereof for advertising or commercial purposes. Some courts have found that commercial use of flags violates flag-desecration statutes even though those statutes contain no specific provisions against commercial use.

Courtroom Proceedings

In 1937, the American Bar Association adopted Canon 35 of the Canons of Judicial Ethics prohibiting broadcast and photographic coverage of court proceedings. As far as the federal courts are concerned, Rule 53 of the Federal Rules of Criminal Procedure prohibits "taking of photographs in the courtroom during the progress of judicial proceedings."

Generally speaking, the propriety of granting or denying permission to the media to broadcast, record, or photograph court proceedings involves weighing the constitutional guarantees of freedom of the press and the right to a public trial on the one hand, and, on the other hand, the due process rights of the defendant and the power of the courts to control their proceedings in order to permit the fair and impartial administration of justice.

There appears to be general agreement that representatives of the media have a constitutional right to broadcast, record, or photograph court proceedings. However, in cases in which media representatives have claimed that court rules and orders prohibiting broadcast or photographic coverage of judicial proceedings infringed upon the freedom of the press, the prohibitions have been upheld as reasonable and proper attempts to preserve courtroom decorum and to protect the rights of defendants. The courts have also rejected claims by press representatives that such prohibitions deprived them of rights protected by federal civil rights laws.

There also appears to be general agreement that the constitutional right to a public trial does not give the press the right to broadcast, record, or photograph court proceedings, since the right to a public trial is for the benefit of the defendant, and since the requirement of a public trial is satisfied when members of the press and public are permitted to attend a trial and to report what transpires. In a number of cases, the courts have held that court orders prohibiting broadcast or photographic coverage of criminal trials were proper attempts to protect the rights of defendants, and that the orders therefore did not deny the defendants their right to a public trial.

The Supreme Court ruled in *Chandler v. Florida* that the due process rights of an accused are not inherently denied by television coverage, and that no constitutional rule specifically prohibits the states from permitting broadcast or photographic coverage of criminal trial proceedings. The Court pointed out, however, that, depending upon the circumstances under which such coverage takes place, a due process violation might result.

A number of states have permitted such coverage on either a permanent or experimental basis. Therefore, the photographer is advised to consult the applicable rules in order to determine the specific types of equipment which may be permitted, the location of the equipment in the courtroom, and the number of media representatives who may be permitted access to the courtroom to operate such equipment.

Court rules frequently prescribe the specific conditions under which representatives of the media may use broadcasting, recording, or photographic to record judicial proceedings. The courts generally have reasoned that a complete prohibition against broadcast or photographic coverage is not required in order to protect the rights of trial participants or the dignity of court proceedings, and that such coverage does in fact serve the public interest.

Chapter 5

ORGANIZING AS A BUSINESS

One of the reasons—perhaps the primary reason—why photographers like their work is that they feel they have escaped the stultifying atmosphere of the dress-for-success business world. But they have not escaped it entirely. The same laws that govern the billion-dollar auto industry govern the photographer. This being the case, you might as well learn how you can use some of those laws to your advantage.

Any professional person knows that survival requires careful financial planning. Yet few photographers realize the importance of selecting the form of their business. Most photographers have little need for the sophisticated organizational structures utilized in industry, but since photographers must pay taxes, obtain loans, and expose themselves to potential liability every time they take photographs and sell their work, it only makes sense to structure the business so as to minimize these concerns.

Every business has an organizational form best suited to it. When I counsel photographers on organizing their businesses, I usually go about it in two steps. First, we discuss various aspects of taxes and liability in order to decide which of the basic forms is best. There are only a handful of basic forms: *the sole proprietorship*, *the partnership*, *the corporation*, and a few hybrids. Then, once we have decided which of these is appropriate, we go into the organizational details such as partnership agreements or corporate bylaws. These documents define the day-to-day operations of a business and therefore must be tailored to individual situations.

What I offer here is an explanation of features of the various kinds of business organizations, including their advantages and disadvantages. This should give you some idea of which form might be best for you.

I will discuss potential problems, but, since I cannot go into a full discussion of the more intricate details, you should consult an attorney before deciding to adopt any particular structure. My purpose here is to facilitate your communication with your lawyer and to better enable you to understand the choices offered.

The American Dream: Sole Proprietorship

The technical name *sole proprietorship* may be unfamiliar to you, but chances are you are operating under this form now. The sole proprietorship is an unincorporated business owned by one person. Though not peculiar to the United States, it was, and still is, the backbone of the American dream, to the extent that personal freedom follows economic freedom. As a form of business it is elegant in its simplicity. All it requires is a little money and a little work. Legal requirements are few and simple. In most localities, professionals such as photographers are not required to have a business license, but, if you wish to operate the business under a name other than your own, the name must be registered with the state and, in some cases, the county in which you are doing business. With this detail taken care of, you are in business.

Disadvantages of Sole Proprietorship

There are many financial risks involved in operating your business as a sole proprietor. If you recognize any of these dangers as a real threat, you probably should consider an alternative form of organization.

If you are the sole proprietor of a business venture, your personal property is at stake. In other words, if for any reason you owe more than the dollar value of your business, your creditors can force a sale of most of your personal property to satisfy the debt. Thus, if one of your photographs is defamatory, an invasion of someone's privacy, or infringement of a copyright, you could find that you are financially responsible for paying judgment.

For many risks, you can get insurance which will shift the loss from you to an insurance company, but there is no insurance against a sudden rise in the cost of supplies or raw materials such as film or darkroom chemicals. In any case, insurance policies do have monetary limits. Furthermore, insurance premiums can be quite high, and there is no way to accurately predict or plan for future increases in premiums. These hazards, as well as many other uncertain economic factors, can drive a small business into bankruptcy, and that, in turn, could force you into personal bankruptcy if you are the sole proprietor.

Taxes for the Sole Proprietor

The sole proprietor is taxed on all profits of the business and may deduct losses. Of course, the rate of taxation will fluctuate with changes in income. A particularly successful year can leave the sole proprietor no better off financially than in the less successful years, due to the higher tax bracket.

Fortunately, there are ways to ease this tax burden. For instance, you can establish an approved IRA or pension plan, deducting a specified amount of your net income for placement into the pension plan, or into an interest-bearing account, or into approved government securities or mutual funds to be withdrawn later when you are in a lower tax bracket. There are severe restrictions, however, on withdrawal of this money prior to retirement age.

For further information on these tax-planning devices, you should contact your local IRS office and ask for free pamphlets on the Keogh Plan. Or you might wish to use the services of an accountant experienced in dealing with photographers' tax problems.

Partnership

Two photographers can form a partnership. This arrangement can be very attractive to beginning photographers because it allows them to pool their money, equipment, and contacts.

When a photographer agrees to work with another on a project or when a photographer and writer get together and agree to produce a manuscript accompanied by photographs, this also constitutes a partnership. A *partnership* is defined by most state laws as an association of two or more persons to conduct, as co-owners, a business for profit. No formalities are required. In fact, in some cases people have been held to be partners even though they never had any intention of forming a partnership. For example, if you lend a friend some money to start a business and the friend agrees to pay you a certain percentage of whatever profit is made, you may be your friend's partner in the eyes of the law even though you take

no part in running the business. This is important because each partner is subject to unlimited personal liability for the debts of the partnership. Also, each partner is liable for the negligence of another partner and of the partnership's employees when a negligent act occurs in the usual course of business.

This means that if you are getting involved in a partnership as, for example, when you collaborate with someone on a book, you should be careful in three areas. First, since the involvement of a partner increases your potential liability, you must choose a responsible partner. Second, the partnership should be adequately insured to protect both the assets of the partnership and the personal assets of each partner. Finally, it is a good idea for you to draw up a written agreement between you and your partner in order to avoid any misunderstandings or confusion in the future.

As I have already mentioned, no formalities are required to create a partnership. If the partners do not have a formal agreement defining the terms of the partnership—such as control of the partnership or the distribution of profits—state law will determine the legal relationship between the parties. The most important characteristics of this relationship, in the absence of a written partnership agreement, are:

1. No one can become a member of a partnership without the unanimous consent of all partners,

2. All members have an equal vote in the management of the partnership regardless of the size of their interest in it,

3. All partners share equally in the profits and losses of the partnership no matter how much capital they have contributed,

4. A simple majority vote is required for decisions in the ordinary course of business, and a unanimous vote is required to change the fundamental character of the business, and

5. A partnership is terminable at will by any partner; a partner can withdraw from the partnership at any time, and this withdrawal will cause a dissolution of the partnership.

Most state laws contain a provision that allows the partners to make their own agreements regarding the management structure and division of profits that best suits the needs of the individual partners.

What You Don't Want: Unintended Partners

One arrangement you want to avoid is the unintended partnership. This can occur when you collaborate on a work with another person and your relationship is not described formally in a written agreement. Thus, if you do the photography for a corporate report, and ask a friend to provide supplementary photographs, it is essential for you to spell out in detail the arrangements between you and the other person. If you do not, you could find that the other photographer is your partner and entitled to half of the income you receive even though the contribution was minimal. You can avoid this by making an outright purchase of the other person's work or pay that person a percentage of what you are paid. Whichever arrangement you choose, you will be well advised to have a detailed written agreement prepared by an experienced business lawyer.

The Corporation

The corporation may sound like a form of business that pertains only to large companies with many employees—an impersonal monster wholly alien to the world of the photographer. In fact, there is nothing in the nature of a corporation itself that requires it to be large or impersonal. In many states, even one person can incorporate a business. There are advantages and disadvantages to incorporating; if it appears advantageous to incorporate, you will find it can be done with surprising ease and with little expense. However, you will need a lawyer's assistance to ensure that you can comply with state formalities and learn how to use the corporate machinery and pay the corporation's taxes.

Differences between a Corporation and Partnership

To discuss the corporation, it is useful to compare it to a partnership. Perhaps the most important difference is that, like limited partners, the owners of the corporation—commonly known as shareholders or stockholders—are not personally liable for the corporation's debts; they stand to lose only their investment. But unlike a limited partner, a shareholder is allowed full participation in the control of the corporation through the shareholders' voting privileges.

For the small corporation, however, limited liability may be something of an illusion because very often creditors will demand that the owners personally cosign for any credit extended. In addition, individuals remain responsible for their wrongful acts; thus, a photographer who infringes a copyright or creates a defamatory work will remain personally liable even if incorporated. Nevertheless, the corporate liability shield does protect a photographer in situations where a contract is breached and the other contracting party has agreed to look only to the corporation for responsibility. For example, publishing contracts frequently require photographers to make certain guarantees and statements of fact. If the publisher will contract with the photographer's corporation, rather than with the photographer as an individual, then the corporation alone will be liable if there is a breach.

The corporate shield also offers protection in situations where an employee of the photographer has committed a wrongful act while working for the photographer's corporation. If, for example, an assistant negligently injures a pedestrian while the assistant is driving to the store to pick up some film for the photographer, the assistant will be liable for the wrongful act and the corporation may be liable, but the photographer who owns the corporation will probably not be personally liable.

The second area of difference between the corporation and the partnership is in continuity of existence. The many events which can cause the dissolution of a partnership do not have the same result when they occur to a corporation. It is common to create a corporation so that it will have perpetual existence. Unlike partners, shareholders cannot decide to withdraw and demand a return of capital from the corporation; all they can do is sell their stock. Therefore a corporation may have both legal and economic continuity. But this can also be a tremendous disadvantage to shareholders or their heirs if they want to sell their stock but cannot find anyone who wants to buy it. However, there are agreements which may be used to guarantee a return of capital should the shareholder die or wish to withdraw.

The third difference is the free transferability of ownership. In a partnership, no one can become a partner without unanimous consent of the other partners unless otherwise agreed. In a corporation, however, shareholders can generally sell their shares, or any number of them, to whomever they wish. If a small corporation does not want to be open to outside ownership, transferability may be restricted.

The fourth difference is in the structure of management and control. Common shareholders are given a vote in proportion to their ownership in the corporation. Other kinds of stock can be created that may or may not have voting rights. A voting shareholder uses the vote to elect a board of directors and to create rules under which the board will operate.

The basic rules of the corporation are stated in the articles of incorporation, which are filed with the state. These serve as a sort of constitution and can be amended by shareholder vote. More detailed operational rules—bylaws—should also be prepared. Both shareholders and directors may have the power to create or amend bylaws. This varies from state to state and may be determined by the shareholders themselves. The board of directors then makes operational decisions for the corporation and might delegate day-to-day control to a president.

A shareholder, even one who owns all the stock, may not act against a decision of the board of directors. If the board has exceeded the powers granted it by the articles or bylaws, any shareholder may use the courts to fight the decision. But if the board is acting within its powers, the shareholders have no recourse except to remove the board or any board member. In a few more progressive states, a small corporation may entirely forego having a board of directors. In such cases, the corporation is authorized to allow the shareholders to vote on business decisions just as in a partnership.

The fifth distinction between a partnership and a corporation is the corporation's greater variety of ways of raising additional capital. Partnerships are quite restricted in this regard; they can borrow money or, if all the partners agree, they can take on additional partners. A corporation, on the other hand, may issue more stock, and this stock can be of many different varieties: recallable at a set price, for example, or convertible into another kind of stock.

A means frequently used to attract a new investor is to issue preferred stock. This means that the corporation agrees to pay the preferred shareholder some predetermined amount before it pays any dividends to other shareholders. It also means that if the corporation should go bankrupt, the preferred shareholder will be paid out of the proceeds of liquidation before the common shareholders are paid, although after the corporation's creditors are paid.

The issuance of new stock merely requires, in most cases, approval by a majority of the existing shareholders. In addition, corporations can borrow money on a short-term basis by issuing notes, or for a longer period by issuing debentures or bonds. In fact, a corporation's ability to raise additional capital is limited only by its lawyer's creativity and the economics of the marketplace.

The last distinction is the manner in which a corporation is taxed. Under both state and federal laws the profits of the corporation are taxed to the corporation before they are paid out as dividends. Then, because the dividends constitute income to the shareholders, they are taxed again as personal income. This double taxation constitutes the major disadvantage of incorporating.

Avoiding Double Taxation of Corporate Income

There are several methods of avoiding double taxation. First, a corporation can plan its business so as not to show very much profit. This can be done by drawing off what would be profit in payments to shareholders for a variety of services. For example, a shareholder can be paid a salary, rent for property leased to the corporation, or interest on a loan made to the corporation. All of these are legal deductions from the corporate income.

The corporation can also get larger deductions for the various health and retirement benefits provided for its employees than can an individual or a partnership. For example, a corporation can deduct all of its payments made for an employee health plan while at the same time the employee does not pay any personal income tax on this. Sole proprietors or partnerships can only deduct a much smaller portion of these expenses.

The corporation can also reinvest its profits for reasonable business expansion. This undistributed money is not taxed as income to the individual as it would be if earned by a partnership, which does not distribute it.

Reinvestment has at least two advantages. First, the business can be built up with money which has been taxed only at the corporate level. Second, the owner can delay the liquidation and distribution of corporate assets until a time of lower personal income and therefore possibly lower personal taxes.

Subchapter S Corporation

Congress has created a hybrid organizational form which allows the owners of a small corporation to take advantage of many of the features described above in order to avoid the double-taxation problem. This form of organization is called a *Subchapter S corporation*. If the corporation meets certain requirements, which many small businesses do, the owners can elect to be taxed as a partnership. This can be particularly advantageous in the early years of a corporation because the owners of an S corporation can deduct the losses of the corporation from their personal income, whereas they cannot do that in a standard corporation. They can have this favorable tax situation while simultaneously enjoying the corporation's limited-liability status.

Precautions for Minority Shareholders

Dissolving a corporation is not only painful because of certain tax penalties, it is almost always impossible without the consent of the majority of the shareholders. If you are forming a corporation and will be a minority holder you must realize that the majority will have ultimate and absolute control un-less minority shareholders take certain precautions from the start. I could relate numerous horror stories of what some majority shareholders have done to minority shareholders. Avoiding these problems is no more difficult than drafting a sort of partnership agreement among the shareholders. I recommend that you retain your own attorney to represent you during the corporation's formation rather than waiting until it is too late.

It is important for you as a business person to determine which form of organization will be most advantageous for you. This can best be done by consulting with an experienced business lawyer and having your situation evaluated.

Chapter 6

KEEPING TAXES LOW

Photographers rarely think of themselves as being engaged in a business; many, in fact, go to great lengths to avoid feeling involved in the world of commerce. The IRS, however, treats the professional photographer like anyone else in business; thus the photographer has many of the same tax concerns as any other business person. In addition, most photographers have some special tax problems.

First, most professional photographers do not work for a fixed wage or salary; as a result, a photographer's income can fluctuate radically from one tax year to the next. (This is true too, of course, for the photographer who works for someone else but also freelances.) Second, many tax rules designed to facilitate investment are not useful to photographers. Photographers can, however, benefit from certain provisions of the Internal Revenue Code to reduce their income tax liability.

Record-keeping

In order to take advantage of all the tax laws that are favorable to you, it is imperative that you keep good business records. The Internal Revenue Service does not require that you keep any particular type of records. It will be satisfied so long as your record-keeping clearly reflects your income and is consistent over time so that it can make accurate comparisons from year to year when evaluating your income.

The first step in keeping business records that will allow you to maximize your deductions is to open a checking account for your business. Try to pay all your business expenses by check. Be sure to fill in the amount, date, and reason for each check on the stub. If the check was written for an expense related to a particular client or job, be sure to put the client's name or a job number on both the check and the stub. Finally, keep all of your cancelled checks.

Second, file for a taxpayer identification number. In most states and in some cities, photography is a business subject to sales tax. You will need to get in touch with your state and city sales tax bureaus to ascertain their requirements. Usually, the bureau will issue you a taxpayer identification number after you fill out some forms. Then you can buy certain equipment and supplies without paying the sales tax. However, you will later have to act as an agent of the state, collecting sales tax from your clients and paying it to the state. You should be aware that even if you do not collect the sales tax from your customers, you will be liable for paying it.

Third, keep an expense diary which is similar in form to a date book. You should use your expense diary on a daily basis, noting all cash outlays, such as business-related cab fare, tolls, tips, emergency supplies, as they occur. This will satisfy the IRS requirement that you have both a receipt and good evidence of the business purpose for any expenses greater than $25.

Qualifying for Business Deductions

There are two principal ways of reducing tax liability. First, there are significant deductions available to photographers. Second, as I will discuss later in this chapter, photographers can spread their taxable income (and thus reduce their tax liability) by using several provisions in the tax code.

Professional photographers may deduct their business expenses and thereby significantly reduce their taxable income. However, as with other artists and craftspeople, photographers must be able to establish that they are engaged in a trade or business and not merely a personal hobby. You must keep full and accurate records. Receipts are a necessity. Furthermore, it would be best if you had, in addition to a separate checking account, a complete set of books for all of the activities of your trade or business. A dilettante is not entitled to trade or business deductions.

Tax laws presume that a photographer is engaged in a business or trade, as opposed to a hobby, if a net profit results from the photography during three out of the five consecutive years ending with the taxable year in question. If the photographer has not had three profitable years in the last five, the IRS may contend that the photographer is merely indulging in a hobby, in which case the photographer will have to prove *profit motive* in order to claim business expenses. Proof of profit motive does not require the photographer to prove that there was some chance a profit would actually be made; it requires proof only that the photographer intended to make a profit.

The Treasury Regulations call for an objective standard on the profit-motive issue, so statements of the photographer as to intent will not suffice as proof. The regulations list nine factors to be used in determining profit motive:

- The manner in which the taxpayer carries on the activity (i.e., effective business routines and bookkeeping procedures);

- The expertise of the taxpayer or the taxpayer's advisors (i.e., taking courses in appropriate subjects, awards, prior sales or exhibitions, critical recognition, membership in professional organizations, etc.);

- The time and effort expended in carrying on the activity (i.e., at least several hours a day, preferably on a regular basis);

- Expectation that business assets will increase in value (a factor that is of little relevance to the photographer);

- The success of the taxpayer in similar or related activities (i.e., past successes, either financial or critical, even if prior to the relevant five-year period);

- History of income or losses with respect to the activity (i.e., increases in receipts from year to year unless losses vastly exceed receipts over a long period of time);

- The amount of profits, if any, which are earned;

- Financial status (wealth sufficient to support a hobby would weigh against the profit motive);

- Elements of personal pleasure or recreation (i.e., if significant traveling is involved and few photographs produced, the court may be suspicious of profit motive).

No single factor will determine the results. The case of *Young v. United States* provides an example of how the factors are used. Young was a psychoanalyst who also had a photography business. Although Young was not a commercial photographer and she had had large, serious losses, the court held that she had a genuine profit motive in pursuing photography. The court was influenced by the fact that Young did not appear to be pursuing the occupation of photography for mere pleasure or social prestige and that she was organized as a business and kept conventional business records.

Deductible Expenses

Once you have established yourself as engaged in photography as a business, all your ordinary and necessary expenditures for professional photography are deductible business expenses. This would include photographic equipment and supplies, office equipment, research or professional books and magazines, travel for business purposes, certain conference fees, agent commissions, postage, legal fees, accounting fees, and work space. Work space as a deductible expense—particularly space in one's home, which is a matter of concern to numerous business people including photographers—is covered in the next chapter.

Most of a photographer's expenses are classified as *current expenses*: items with a useful life of less than one year. For example, film and supplies, postage, modeling fees, and telephone bills would be current expenses. These expenses are fully deductible in the year incurred.

There are some business expenses, however, that cannot be fully deducted in the year of purchase but must be depreciated or amortized. These costs are *capital expenditures*. For example, the cost of professional equipment such as a camera or lighting equipment, which have a useful life of more than one year, are capital expenditures and cannot be fully deducted in the year of purchase. Instead, the taxpayer has to depreciate, or allocate, the cost of the item over the estimated useful life of the asset. This is sometimes referred to as *capitalizing* or amortizing the cost. Although the actual useful life of professional equipment will vary, fixed periods have been established in the Code over which depreciation may be deducted.

In some cases it may be difficult to decide whether an expense is a capital expenditure or a current expense. Repairs to equipment are one example. If you spend $200 servicing a camera, this expense may or may not constitute a capital expenditure. The general test is whether the amount spent restoring the equipment has added to its value or substantially prolonged its useful life. Since the cost of replacing short-lived parts of equipment to keep it in efficient working condition does not substantially add to the useful life of equipment, such a cost would be a current cost and would be deductible. The cost of reconditioning equipment, on the other hand, significantly extends its useful life. Thus, such a cost is a capital expenditure and would have to be depreciated or amortized.

Unfortunately, the 1986 tax law modified the rule on deductions for photographers, writers, and other creative people. The so-called "uniform amortization rule" provides that a photographer may only deduct the cost of a particular project in the year incurred if that project is sold within the same year. Thus, a photographer would have to determine which costs are attributable to a particular photograph, and those costs *must* be amortized until the photo is sold, unless the photograph is sold during the year in which the costs were incurred. Professional associations lobbied Congress to change this rule for photographers, writers, and artists. It has been speculated that if a rule such as this had been in force during the American Civil War, no photographic record of the conflict would have survived, since photographers would not have been willing to take photos which might not have sold in the same year.

In 1988, the uniform amortization rule was repealed for writers, photographers, and fine artists.

For many small businesses, an immediate deduction can be taken when equipment is purchased. Beginning in 1987, up to $10,000 of such purchases may be "expensed" each year, and need not be depreciated at all. This is called the "election to depreciate certain business assets." In order to take advantage of the provision, you must have net income of at least the amount of the deduction.

Commissions paid to agents, as well as fees paid to lawyers or accountants for business purposes, are generally deductible as current expenses. The same is true of salaries paid to assistants and others whose services are necessary for the photography business. If you need to hire help, it is a good idea to hire people on an individual-project basis as independent contractors rather than as regular employees. This way, you do not have to pay for social security, disability, and withholding tax. You must file a form 1099 for independent contractors who earn $600 or more per year. When hiring an independent contractor, specify the job-by-job basis of the assignments, detail when each project is to be completed and, if possible,

allow the person you are hiring to choose the place to do the work (since this might underscore the person's independence).

Travel, Entertainment, and Conventions

Many photographers travel abroad in order to shoot certain subjects. Even more commonly, a photographer might travel in the U.S.

On a business trip, whether within the U.S. or abroad, ordinary and necessary expenses are deductible if the travel is solely for business purposes. Transportation costs are fully deductible, except for "luxury water travel," as are costs of lodging while away from home on business. Note, however, that beginning in 1987, only 80 percent of the costs of business meals, and meals consumed while on a business trip, are deductible.

If the trip is primarily for business, but part of the time is given to a personal vacation, you must indicate which expenses are for business and which for pleasure. This is *not* true in the case of foreign trips if one of the following exceptions applies:

> You had no control over arranging the trip,
>
> The trip outside of the U.S. was for a week or less,
>
> You are not a managing executive or shareholder of the company that employed you.

If you are claiming one of these exceptions you should be careful to have supporting documentation. If you cannot take advantage of one of the exceptions, then you must allocate expenses for the trip abroad according to the percentage of the trip devoted to business versus vacation.

Whether inside or outside of the U.S., the definition of what constitutes a business day can be very helpful to the taxpayer in determining a trip's deductibility. Travel days, including the day of departure and the day of return, count as business days if business activities occurred on such days. If travel is outside the U.S., the same rules apply if the foreign trip is for more than seven days. *Any day which the taxpayer spends on business counts as a business day even if only a part of the day is spent on business.* A day in which business is canceled through no fault of the taxpayer counts as a business day. Saturdays, Sundays, and holidays count as business days even though no business is conducted, provided that business is conducted on the Friday before and the Monday after the weekend, or one day on either side of the holiday.

Entertainment expenses incurred for the purpose of developing an existing business are also deductible, in the amount of 80 percent of the actual cost. However, you must be especially careful about recording entertainment expenses. You should record in your logbook the amount, date, place, type of entertainment, business purpose, substance of the discussion, the participants in the discussion, and the business relationship of the parties who are being entertained. Keep receipts for any expenses over $25. You should also keep in mind the new stipulation in the tax code which disallows deductibility for expenses which are "lavish or extravagant under the circumstances." No guidelines have yet been developed as to the definition of "lavish or extravagant," but you should be aware of the restriction nevertheless. If tickets to a sporting, cultural, or other event are purchased, only the face value of the ticket is allowed as a deduction. If a skybox or other luxury box seat is purchased or leased and is used for business entertaining, the maximum deduction now allowed is the cost of a non-luxury box seat.

The above rules cover business travel and entertainment expenses both inside and outside of the United States. The rules are more stringent for deducting expenses incurred while attending conventions and conferences outside the United States. Also, the IRS tends to review very carefully any deductions for attendance at business seminars that also involve a family vacation, whether inside the U.S. or abroad. In order to deduct the business expense, the taxpayer must be able to show, with documents, that the reason for attending the meeting was to promote production of income. Normally, for a spouse's expenses to be deductible, the spouse's presence must be required by the photographer's employer. In the case of an independent photographer who has organized into a partnership or small corporation, it is wise, if the spouse will also be going on business trips, to make the spouse a partner, employee, or member of the board of the company. Often, seminars will offer special activities for husbands and wives that will provide documentation later on.

As a general rule, the business deductions are for conventions and seminars held in North America. The IRS is taking a closer look at cruise-ship seminars and is now requiring two statements to be attached to the tax return when such seminars are involved. The first statement substantiates the number of days on the ship, the number of hours spent each day on business, and the activities in the program. The second statement must come from the sponsor of the convention to verify the first information. In addition, the ship must be registered in the U.S., and all ports of call must be located in the U.S. or its possessions. Again, the key for the taxpayer taking this sort of deduction is careful documentation and substantiation.

Keeping a logbook or expense diary is probably the best line of defense for the photographer with respect to business expenses incurred while traveling. If you are on the road, keep these things in mind:

(1) With respect to travel expenses:
    Keep proof of the costs,
    Record the time of departure,
    Record the number of days spent on
      business,
    List the places visited and the business
      purposes of your activities.
(2) With respect to the transportation costs:
    Keep copies of all receipts in excess of $25,
    If traveling by car, keep track of mileage, and
    Log all other expenses in your diary.

Similarly, with meals, tips, and lodging, keep receipts for all items over $25 and make sure to record all less-expensive items in your logbook.

Photographers may also take tax deductions for their attendance at workshops, seminars, retreats, and the like, provided that they are careful to document the business nature of the trip. Accurate record-keeping is the first line of defense for tax preparation.

Charitable Deductions

The law regarding charitable deductions by creative people of their own work is not very advantageous. Individuals who donate items they have created may only deduct the cost of materials used to create those works. This provision has had unfortunate effects on libraries and museums, which, since the law's passage in 1969, have experienced enormous decreases in charitable contributions from authors, artists, and craftspeople. The Museum of Modern Art, for example, received fifty-two paintings and sculptures from artists from 1967 to 1969; between 1972 and 1975, only one work was donated.

The current tax law puts a further barrier in the way of charitable donations by requiring that a deduction may be taken only by those who itemize. The previous law allowed a charitable deduction whether the taxpayer took the standard deduction or itemized.

Although several modifications of the law have

been proposed, Congress continues to resist change in the area of tax treatment regarding individuals' donations of their own work. However, some states have been more responsive. Oregon and Kansas now allow creators to deduct the fair market value of their creations donated to qualified charities, and California treats creative property as a capital asset.

Grants, Prizes, and Awards

Those photographers who receive income from grants or fellowships should be aware that this income can be excluded from gross income and thus represents considerable tax savings. To qualify for this exclusion the grant must be for the purpose of furthering the photographer's education and training. If the grant is given as compensation for services or is primarily for the benefit of the grant-giving organization, it cannot be excluded. Amounts received under a grant or fellowship that are specifically designated to cover related expenses for the purpose of the grant are no longer fully deductible.

For scholarships and fellowships granted after August 16, 1986, the above deductions are allowed only if the recipient is a degree candidate, and the amount of the exclusion from income is limited to the amounts used for tuition, fees, books, supplies and equipment. Amounts designated for room, board, and other incidental expenses are considered to be income. No exclusions from income are allowed for recipients who are not degree candidates.

The above rules apply to income from grants and fellowships. Unfortunately, the Tax Reform Act of 1986 also put tighter restrictions on money, goods, or services received as prizes or awards. Previously, the amounts received for certain awards were excluded from income in certain cases where the recipient was rewarded for past achievements, and had not applied for the award. Under the Tax Reform Act of 1986, any prizes or awards for charitable, scientific, or artistic achievements are included as income to the recipient, unless the prize is assigned to charity.

Income in Installments and Deferred Payments

In addition to taking all possible deductions, a photographer can spread income by receiving payment in installments. Care must be taken with the mechanics of this arrangement, however. If a photographer sells photographs for a negotiable note due in full at some future date, or for some other deferred-payment obligation that is essentially equivalent to

cash or has an ascertainable fair market value, the photographer may have to report the total proceeds of the sale as income realized when the note is received, not when the note is paid off with cash. However, if you sell property and receive payments in successive tax years, the Internal Revenue Code allows you to report the income on an installment basis. Under this method, tax is imposed only as payments are received.

For example, suppose you sell a series of photographs for $3,000. Ordinarily the entire $3,000 would be taxable income in the year you received it. But if you use the installment method, with four payments of $750 plus interest received annually over four years, income from the sale will be taxed as the installments are received. In either case, the amount of income is $3,000, but under the installment method the amount is spread out over four years. This could put you in a lower tax bracket than you would have been in had you taken the full $3,000 in the year you sold your photographs.

Photographers in high tax brackets may wish to defer income until the future. To do this, a photographer could agree in a contract that payments will not exceed a certain amount in any one year, with excess payments to be carried over and paid in the future. This would result in tax savings if, when the deferred amounts are finally paid, the photographer is in a lower tax bracket.

There are drawbacks to deferred payments which include the possibility that your client may not be willing to pay interest on the deferred sums, or the possibility that the client could go broke before you are fully paid. You should consider these risks carefully before entering into a contract for deferred payments, because it might be quite difficult to change the arrangement if the need should arise.

Spreading Income Among a Family

Another strategy for photographers is to divert some of their income directly to members of their immediate family who are in lower tax brackets by hiring them as employees. Putting dependent children on the payroll can result in a substantial tax savings for professional photographers because they can deduct the salaries as a business expense and, as of 1988, they are not responsible for withholding social security from their children's wages.

Your child can earn up to $4,440 in 1988 without any tax liability, taking into account the $3,000 standard deduction and the $1,950 personal exemption. In 1989 the standard deduction will be $3,000 adjusted for inflation and the personal exemption will be $2,000. Under the Internal Revenue Code of 1986, however, the child may not claim the personal exemption if he or she can be claimed by the parents on their tax return.

There are some restrictions on such an arrangement:

1. The salary must be reasonable in relation to the child's age and the work performed;

2. The work performed must be a necessary service to the business; and

3. The work must actually be performed by the child.

A second method of transferring income to members of your family is the creation of a family partnership. Each partner is entitled to receive an equal share of the overall income, unless the partnership agreement provides otherwise. The income is taxed once as individual income to each partner. Thus, the photographer with a family partnership can break up and divert income to the family members so it will be taxed to them according to their respective tax brackets. The income received by children may be taxed at significantly lower rates, resulting in more income reaching the family than if it had all been received by the photographer, who is presumably in a higher tax bracket than the children. But the Internal Revenue Code of 1986 stipulates that if a child is under fourteen years of age, and receives unearned income from the partnership, any amount over $500 will be taxed at the parents' highest marginal rate.

Although the IRS allows family partnerships, it may subject them to close scrutiny to ensure that the partnership is not a sham. Unless the partnership capital is a substantial income-producing factor and unless partners are reasonably compensated for services performed on the partnership's behalf, the IRS may, in applying the section of the Code which deals with distribution of partners' shares and family partnerships, decide to forbid the shift in income. This section provides that a person owning a capital interest in a family partnership will be considered a partner for tax purposes even if he or she received the capital interest as a gift. But the gift must be genuine, and it should not be revocable.

Incorporating a Family

In the past, some families incorporated in order to take advantage of the then more favorable corporate tax rates. If the IRS questioned the motivation

for such an incorporation, the courts examined the intent of the family members, and if the sole purpose of incorporating was tax avoidance, the scheme was disallowed.

The Tax Reform Act of 1986 reduced the individual income tax rates so that, for most taxpayers, they are substantially in line with or lower than the tax imposed on corporations. There may, therefore, no longer be substantial tax benefit in incorporating a business. There may, however, be other reasons for incorporating, as, for example, to obtain limited liability as discussed in Chapter 5. Similarly, for anyone who teaches photography, taking photographs may be an occupational requirement. A photographer may, therefore, wish to incorporate and elect to be taxed as an S corporation. This will enable the corporation to insulate the photographer from personal liability while permitting the business to be taxed as if it were individually owned. If the photographer employs a spouse and children, salaries paid to them will be considered business deductions and thus reduce the photographer's taxable income. When the spouse and children are made owners of the corporation by being provided with shares of stock in it, all of the benefits discussed in the preceding section on partnership will be available. Note, however, that losses derived from passive investment, such as stock ownership, may be used only to offset earnings from passive investments and may not be deducted against ordinary income. As to the unearned income received from the corporation by a child under fourteen, the same rule applies as unearned income from a family partnership: amounts over $500 are taxed at the parents' highest marginal rate.

* * *

In conclusion, even though many photographers do not consider themselves business persons, they may be taxed as such. Because many of the tax provisions designed to encourage the investment end of business are not available to photographers, you need to concentrate on other methods of reducing taxes. The methods discussed here—various deductions and ways of income spreading—provide you with a starting point for reducing taxes. Be careful to avoid going beyond the realm of accepted tax planning. If a particular activity is questionable, you should consult with a competent CPA or tax advisor before embarking on it. In any case, consultation with competent tax professionals is always advisable to ensure maximum benefits.

Chapter 7

TAX DEDUCTIONS FOR THE OFFICE AT HOME

It is quite common for photographers to have offices, studios, or darkrooms at home for a variety of reasons. The most important reason, though, is probably economic. The cost of renting a separate studio or darkroom is such that many photographers prefer to work at home. Others, of course, choose to work at home because it enables them to juggle work and family. Whatever the reason, photographers who wish to get tax deductions for use of their homes in their business will have to do some careful planning.

The IRS has not always allowed deductions for offices or studios in residences. This situation was challenged in a case regarding a physician who managed rental properties as a sideline. The doctor's rental business was run out of an office in his house, and the space was used only for this particular business. When the physician deducted the expenses for the office in his home, the IRS disallowed the deduction. But the court was apparently convinced by the physical set-up of the room that the doctor used it exclusively and regularly as an office in connection with his rental business. The court noted the room had no television set, sofa, or bed.

This decision has been incorporated into the tax code. As a general rule, a business deduction is not allowed for the use of a dwelling that is used by the taxpayer as a residence. Use as a residence is defined as the use of the unit for personal purposes for more than fourteen days of the taxable year. But the statute does allow the taxpayer to take a deduction for a portion of a dwelling unit "exclusively used on a regular basis ... as a principal place of business for any trade or business of the taxpayer," even if that business is not the taxpayer's primary source of income.

Exclusive and Regular Use

The exclusive and regular use exception applies to any portion of the residence used *exclusively* and *on a regular basis* as the photographer's *principal place of business*.

The qualifications for this exception are strictly construed by the IRS and the courts. The requirement of exclusivity means that the taxpayer may not mix personal use and business use; in other words, an office that doubles as a storeroom for personal belongings, a laundry room, or the like will not qualify as an office for tax purposes, and a taxpayer may not deduct such space as an office.

However, there has been a recent liberalization of this rule in some parts of the country where the courts have held that a studio or an office can exist in a room that has a personal use, so long as a clearly defined area is used exclusively for business. It is important to remember that generally the Internal Revenue Service functions on a regional basis. Except for issues that have been reserved for decision by the national office, each IRS office is autonomous and makes its own decisions until the United States Supreme Court or Congress makes a decision that applies nationally. That is why the decision by a lower court in one area may not apply elsewhere.

The requirement regarding regular use means that the use of the room may not be merely incidental or occasional. Obviously, there is a gray area between regular and occasional. Perhaps some photographers can use this rule as an inducement to overcome temporary bouts of laziness or ennui. For if you as a photographer are planning on deducting any expenses for your office, you must keep working to satisfy the regularity test.

What If the Photographer Also Works Elsewhere?

Like the regularity requirement, the rule regarding the principal place of business has been very vague. However, under IRS interpretations, a taxpayer may have a different principal place of business for each trade or business in which that person is engaged. The test requires looking at the particular facts of each case, but generally the key elements are (1) the amount of income derived from the business done there, (2) the amount of time spent there, and (3) the nature of the facility.

Thus it is now possible, for example, for an elementary or secondary school teacher, whose principal place of business (judging by income and time spent) is a school, to also run a sideline business of photography out of the home and to claim the office in the home as the principal place of business for the photography enterprise. In situations such as this, the courts have also recognized another element: practical necessity. A teacher has a legitimate reason for deducting for space used at home.

Perhaps a more common case would be a photographer working elsewhere as a photographer, for example, on a newspaper. This woman hopes to eventually support herself as a commercial photographer working on her own, and in the meantime uses her spare time to build a reputation and produce work from her home. Would the IRS allow her to take deductions for office/studio space at home when she does have access to the newspaper's facilities? Yes; again practical necessity exists, since the newspaper's equipment is obviously not for her personal use.

A third situation might arise when a photographer hopes to make deductions for work space at home even though his employer provides work space. In this case it would be necessary to show that the home space is needed because of a specific IRS requirement: "for the convenience of the employer." Again, necessity is an important consideration.

In a similar situation in *Frankel v. Commissioner*, the court considered the deductibility of an office at home for a *New York Times* editor who continuously and regularly used a specific room in his house for business purposes. The court reasoned that the home office was clearly for the benefit of Frankel's employer, since Frankel could not properly perform his job without the office at home unless he were to go on duty twenty-four hours a day and "sleep on an army cot in his employer's office," because he had to be in constant touch with business contacts all hours of the day and night.

The tax court went on to say, however, that there was one additional requirement. The editor-employee—Frankel—must actually "*meet* with patients, clients or customers" in the office at home. The court was liberal in its interpretation of which individuals would satisfy this criterion for an editor, finding that photographers, political figures, and news sources would be considered clients for purposes of the Internal Revenue Code. Nevertheless, the court found that Frankel did not meet with the clients at the home office but, rather, spoke with them on the telephone. It held that he did not satisfy all of the Internal Revenue Code's requirements.

This reasoning may well be applicable to employee-photographers who find themselves in circumstances similar to Frankel's. For example, if you are a professional photographer who maintains an office at home even though your employer provides work space, *it may be necessary for clients to come to your home office to satisfy the "for the convenience of the employer" test.* If, for an editor, clients are photographers, political figures, and news sources, your clients might be editors, news sources, models, expert consultants, or other people who are involved in whatever you are shooting.

It is not clear what impact the *Frankel* case would have for photographers engaged by an employer who does not supply any office space, so that the only office available is in the photographer's home. The prudent individual will strive to fulfill the *Frankel* criteria even in this situation, by inviting any other people involved in the work to meet with the photographer in the office at home.

When the office is in a structure separate from the principal residence, the requirements for deductibility are less stringent. The structure must be used exclusively and on a regular basis, just as an office in the home itself. However, when the office is in a separate structure, it need only be used "in connection with" the photography business, not as the principal place of business.

When photographers use a portion of their homes for storage of business materials (as well as for business), the requirements for deductibility of the storage area are also less stringent. The dwelling must be the sole fixed location of the business and the storage area must be used on a regular basis for the storage of the photographer's work or equipment. The entire room used for storage need not be used exclusively for business, but there must be a "separately identifiable space suitable for storage" of the photographer's work or work-related materials.

Is the Office-at-Home Deduction Worthwhile?

If a photographer meets one of the tests outlined above, the next question is what tax benefits can result. The answer after close analysis is frequently, "Not very many." An *allocable portion* of mortgage interest and property taxes can be deducted against the business. These would be deductible anyway as itemized deductions. The advantage of deducting them against the business is that this reduces the business profit that is subject to self-employment taxes.

Of course, a taxpayer who lives in a rented house and otherwise qualifies for the office-at-home deductions may deduct a portion of the rent that would not otherwise be tax deductible.

The primary tax advantage comes from a deduction for an allocable portion of repairs, utility bills, and depreciation that otherwise would not be deductible at all.

To arrive at the allocable portion, take the square footage of the space used for the business and divide that by the total square footage of the house. Multiply this fraction by your mortgage interest, property taxes, etc., for the amount to be deducted. How to determine the amount of allowable depreciation is too complex to discuss here, and you should discuss this with your accountant or tax advisor.

The total amount that can be deducted for an office or storage place in the home is limited. To determine the amount that can be deducted, take the total amount of money earned in the business and subtract the allocable portion of mortgage interest and property taxes, and the other deductions allocable to the business. The remainder is the maximum amount that you can deduct for the allocable portion of repairs, utilities, and depreciation. In other words, your total business deductions in this situation cannot be greater than your total business income minus all other business expenses. The home-office deduction, therefore, cannot be used to create a net loss. But disallowed losses can be carried forward and deducted in future years.

Besides the obvious complexity of the rules and the mathematics, there are several other factors that limit the benefit of taking a deduction for a studio or office in the home. One of these is the partial loss of the *nonrecognition of gain* (tax-deferred) treatment that is otherwise allowed when a taxpayer sells a principal residence. Ordinarily, when someone sells a principal residence for profit, the tax on the gain is deferred if the seller purchases another principal residence of at least the same value within two years.

Most of the tax on this gain is never paid during the taxpayer's lifetime.

This deferral of gain, however, is not allowed to the extent that the house was used in the business.

For example, if you have been claiming 20 percent of your home as a business deduction, when you sell the home you will enjoy a tax deferral on only 80 percent of the profit. The other 20 percent will be subject to tax because that 20 percent represents the sale of a business asset.

In essence, for the price of a current deduction you may be converting what is essentially a nonrecognition, or tax-deferred, asset into a trade or business property.

However, there is one important exception that can work to your advantage. The IRS has ruled that *if you stop qualifying* for the office-at-home tax deduction for at least one year before you sell the house, you are entitled to the entire gain as *rollover*, no matter how many years you have been taking the deduction. (A rollover means you can reinvest the proceeds of the sale in another dwelling within the prescribed period and avoid paying taxes.)

The word *qualifying* in the IRS ruling has a very technical meaning. It does not only mean that you stop taking the business deduction for one year. It also means that you physically move the business out of your home so that it no longer qualifies as an office at home, whether or not you have taken it as a tax deduction. The same ruling applies to the one-time tax exemption of up to $125,000 on the sale of a home by persons over age fifty-five. If you plan to sell any time soon, check all this out with an accountant or tax advisor. A little planning might save you a great deal of money.

Alerting the IRS

Another concern is that by deducting for an office in the home, the taxpayer in effect puts a red flag on the tax return. Obviously, when the tax return expressly asks whether expenses are being deducted for an office in the home, the question is not being asked for purely academic reasons. Although only the IRS knows how much the answer to this question affects someone's chances of being audited, there is no doubt that a "yes" answer does increase the likelihood of an audit.

Given this increased possibility of audit, it doesn't pay to deduct for an office in the home in doubtful situations. Taxpayers who lose the deduction must pay back taxes plus interest or fight in court. One unfortunate taxpayer not only lost the deduction on a technicality, but also lost the rollover treatment on the sale of his home.

If you believe that your studio or dark room or office at home could qualify for the business deduction, you would be well advised to consult with a competent tax expert who can assist in calculating the deduction.

Chapter 8

WHAT TO KNOW ABOUT LEASES AND INSURANCE

Leases

At some time in your professional life as a photographer, you will be in a position where you may have to evaluate the terms and conditions of a commercial lease. You may also have to examine a residential lease, although these are customarily more tightly regulated by state law than are commercial leases. The relationship between a landlord and a tenant varies from state to state and it is important for you to consult with a local attorney who has some expertise in dealing with this body of law before signing a lease. As a photographer, however, you may wish to call your attorney's attention to some specific items in a commercial lease which could be of great concern to you.

What the Property and Cost Really Involve

One of the most important terms in any lease is the description of the property to be rented. Be sure that the document specifies, in some detail, the area that you are entitled to occupy. If you will be renting a studio in a building with common areas, you should have the responsibilities for those common areas spelled out. Will you be responsible for cleaning and maintaining them, or will the landlord? When will the common areas be open or closed? What other facilities are available to you, such as restrooms, storage and the like?

Another important item is the cost of the leased space. Will you be paying a flat monthly rental or one which will change based on your earnings at the location? In order to evaluate the cost of the space, you should compare it with other similar spaces in the same locale. Do not be afraid to negotiate for more favorable terms.

Length of the Lease

It is also important to consider the period of the lease. If you intend to rent a studio for a year or two, it is a good idea to try to get an option to extend. It is likely you will want to advertise and promote your business, and if you move on an annual basis, customers may feel that you are unstable. In addition, occasional customers who return on an irregular basis may not know where to find you after the lease period ends. Besides, moving can result in real headaches in regard to mail.

Long-term leases are recordable in some jurisdictions. If you are in a position to record your lease, it is probably a good idea to do so since you will be entitled to receive legal and other notices related to the property.

Restrictions To Watch Out For

It is essential for you to determine whether there are any restrictions on the particular activity you wish to perform at the leased premises. For example, the area may be zoned so that you are prohibited from discharging developing chemicals into the sewer system. It is a good idea to insist on a provision which puts the burden of obtaining any permit or variances on the landlord or, if you are responsible for them, allowing you to terminate the lease without penalty if you cannot get the permits or variances.

Be sure that the lease permits you to display any sign or advertising used in connection with your business. It is not uncommon, for example, for historic landmark laws to regulate signs put on old buildings. Can you put a sign in your window or in front of your building? Some zoning laws prohibit this.

Remodeling and Utilities

Photographers should also be aware that extensive remodeling may be necessary for certain spaces to become useful studios. If this is the case, it is important for you to determine who will be responsible for the costs of remodeling. In addition, it is essential to find out whether it will be necessary for you to restore the premises to their original condition when the lease ends. This can be extraordinarily expensive and, in some instances, impossible to accomplish.

If you need special hookups, such as water or electrical lines, find out whether the landlord will provide them or whether you have to bear the cost of having them brought in. Of course, if the leased premises already have the necessary facilities, question the landlord regarding the cost of these utilities. Are they included in the rent or are they to be paid separately?

In some locations, garbage pickup is not a problem, since it is one of the services provided by the municipality. On the other hand, it is common for renters to be responsible for their own trash disposal. In commercial spaces, this can be quite expensive and should be addressed in the lease.

Insurance, Security and Deliveries

Customarily the landlord will be responsible for the exterior of the building. It will be the landlord's obligation to make sure that it does not leak during rainstorms and that it is properly ventilated. Nevertheless, it is important that the lease deal with the question of responsibility if, for example, the building is damaged and some of your photographs are injured or destroyed. Will you have to take out insurance for the building as well as its contents or will the landlord assume responsibility for building insurance? Similarly, find out whether you will have to get liability insurance for injuries in portions of the building not under your control, such as common hallways and the like. In any case, you should of course have your own liability policy for accidental injuries or accidents that occur on your premises.

A good lease will also contain a provision dealing with security. If you are renting an internal space in a shopping center, it is likely that the landlord will be responsible for external security; this is not universally the case, though, so you should find out about security. If you are renting an entire building, it is customarily your responsibility to provide whatever security you deem important. Does the lease permit you to install locks or alarm systems? If this is something you are going to be interested in, you should get an answer to that question.

Many photographers have materials delivered to their studio at off hours so as to avoid disturbing potential customers. Does the lease have any restrictions regarding time or location of deliveries? If you are dealing with large bulky items and are accepting deliveries or making them, put a provision in your lease that will give you the flexibility you desire.

Zoning: Can You Work and Live There?

If the place you wish to rent will be used as both your personal dwelling and studio, some special problems may arise. It is quite common for zoning laws to prohibit certain forms of commercial activities in dwellings when the area is zoned residential. In an attempt to overcome this problem, the Volunteer Lawyers for the Arts in New York successfully lobbied for a law which would allow artists to work and live in the same space in the Soho district. Similar ordinances and statutes have been enacted in other parts of the country but this is by no means a national trend. You should, therefore, consult with your attorney before attempting to set up a studio in your home or to put a bed in your studio.

Get It in Writing

Finally, it is essential to be sure that every item agreed upon between you and the landlord is reduced to writing. This is particularly important when dealing with leases, since many state laws provide that a long-term lease is an interest in land and can only be enforced if it is in writing.

The relationship between landlords and tenants is an ancient one which is undergoing a good deal of change. Care should be taken when examining a location to determine exactly what you can do on the premises and whether the landlord or municipal rules will allow you to use the location for your specific purpose.

Insurance

As a photographer, you probably will need several types of insurance. Obviously, a camera floater, which is written to cover loss or damage to equipment, is a necessity. The camera floater will probably be attached to some form of package policy which would cover your business premises against fire, theft, or other hazards.

A general liability provision covers you for claims of injury to others resulting from your negligence. Coverage includes bodily injury at or away from the studio. If you do fashion work and have models in your studio on a regular basis, it is important that you carry enough liability insurance to cover them in the event they are injured and become unable to work. You should check your automobile coverage to see if it covers models if they become injured while you transport them to and from work. Liability coverage can be extended to include legal injury, such as invasion of privacy or libel.

In addition, you might consider professional malpractice coverage, which would cover any liability you would incur in a situation where your client sued you because her pictures did not turn out as anticipated. For instance, if you leave the lens cover on the camera while shooting a wedding, malpractice insurance will enable you to compensate your customer and will protect you from what might be a disastrous financial liability.

Also available is bailee coverage, which you might consider if you often photograph the property of others and it remains under your control for a period of time. If you are photographing priceless art objects, one of which becomes broken or lost, bailee coverage could be a godsend.

Also, individuals applying for medical insurance are generally charged extremely high rates. If you join an organization like the American Society of Magazine Photographers, you may be able to take advantage of group rates available to members.

Because a photographer's insurance needs tend to be complicated and tend to vary with the type of photography done, you should try to find an insurance broker experienced in serving photographers.

Chapter 9

BASIC TYPES OF CONTRACTS AND REMEDIES

In the normal course of business, photographers enter into contracts with magazines, agents, other photographers, customers, or film developers. The contractual terms may vary with the kind of service or image contracted for, but in every case the nature of legally binding agreements is the same.

The word *contract* commonly brings to mind a long, complicated document replete with legal jargon designed to provide hours of work for lawyers. But this need not be the case. A simple, straightforward contract can be just as valid and enforceable as a complicated one.

What is a Contract?

A contract is defined as a legally binding promise or set of promises. The law requires the participants in a contract to perform the promises they have made to each other. In the event of non-performance — usually called a *breach* — the law provides remedies to the injured party. For the purposes of this discussion, we will assume that the contract is between two people.

The three basic elements of every contract are the *offer*, the *acceptance*, and the *consideration*. Suppose, for example, you show a potential customer a variety of black-and-white family portraits taken in your studio and suggest what you think would be the best arrangement for photographing her family (the offer). The customer says she likes the way you have photographed other families and wants you to do it the same way for her (the acceptance). You agree on a price (the consideration).

That's the basic framework, but a great many variations can be played on that theme.

Types of Contracts

Contracts may be *express* or *implied*; they may be *oral* or *written*. On this latter point, there are at least two types of contracts that *must* be in writing if they are to be legally enforceable: (1) any contract which, by its terms, cannot be completed in less than one year, and (2) any contract that involves the sale of goods for over $500.

An *express* contract is one in which all the details are spelled out. Suppose, for example, you make a contract with a sculptor to deliver fifty slides of his work, to be delivered on or before October 1, at an agreed-upon price, which will be paid thirty days after the slides are delivered.

That's fairly straightforward. If either party fails to live up to any material part of the contract, a breach has occurred, and the other party may withhold performance of his or her obligation until receiving assurance that the breaching party will perform. In the event no such assurance is forthcoming, the aggrieved party may have reason to take action and go to court for breach of contract.

If the slides are delivered on October 15 and the sculptor had needed to get them to the judges for a juried exhibit by October 10, time was an important consideration and the sculptor would not be required to accept the late delivery. But if time is not a material consideration, then the tardy delivery would probably be considered "substantial performance" and the sculptor would have to accept the delivery in spite of the delay.

Express contracts can be either oral or written, though if you are going to the trouble of expressing contractual terms, you should put your understanding in writing.

Implied contracts need not be very complicated either, though they are usually not done in writing. Suppose you call a printer to order 1,000 sheets of letterhead without making an express statement that you will pay for the printing. The promise to pay is implied in the order, and is enforceable when the stationery is picked up.

But with implied contracts, things can often become a lot stickier. Suppose an acquaintance asks you, a well-known wildlife photographer, to bring over one of your recent large prints of a nesting eagle to see how it will look in her living room. She asks if you would leave it there for a few days. Two months later she still has it, and you overhear her raving to others about how marvelous it looks over the fireplace.

Is there an implied contract to purchase in this arrangement? That may depend on whether you are normally in the business of selling your work, or whether you usually loan your work for approval.

Most contracts that photographers enter into in terms of their work involve some aspect of the sale of that work.

Another kind of implied contract will arise when somebody requests you to send them your work. When, for example, Nike Corporation requested sports-action photographer, Don Johnson, to send his portfolio to the corporation, there was an implied agreement that Nike would take reasonable care of the portfolio and return it in due course. When the portfolio was lost at Nike, Johnson sued and recovered for his lost work.

Let's examine the principles of offer, acceptance, and consideration in the context of several potential situations for a hypothetical freelance photographer, Pat Smith.

Smith has had works accepted in local and regional exhibitions, has won several prizes, and is getting assignments from large national corporations. In a word, Smith is developing quite a reputation. With this brief background, we'll look at the following situations and see whether an enforceable contract comes into existence.

• At a cocktail party, Jones expresses an interest in hiring Smith to photograph Jones's family. "It looks like your work will go up in price pretty soon," Jones tells Smith. "I'm going to hire you while I can still afford you."

Is this a contract? If so, what are the terms of the offer—the particular work, the specific price? No, this is not really an offer that Smith can accept. It is nothing more than an opinion or a vague expression of intent.

• Brown offers to pay $400 for one of Smith's photographs that she saw in a show several months ago. At the show it was listed at $450, but Smith agrees to accept the lower price.

Is this an enforceable contract? Yes! Brown has offered, in unambiguous terms, to pay a specific amount for a specific work, and Smith has accepted the offer. A binding contract exists.

• One day Gray shows up at Smith's studio and sees a photograph which she would like to use in her book. She offers $200 for the exclusive publication rights in the photograph. Smith accepts and promises to deliver the photograph to Gray's publisher next week, at which time Gray will pay for the rights. An hour later, Brown shows up. She likes the same photograph and offers Smith $300 for the exclusive publishing rights in it. Can Smith accept the later offer?

No—a contract exists with Jones. An offer was made and accepted. The fact that the rights have not yet been exercised or paid for does not make the contract any less binding.

• Green agrees that Smith will photograph Green's wedding and present Green with an acceptable wedding album for $1,000. It is understood that Smith will take a variety of shots throughout the festivities. After Smith presents Green with the proofs, Green indicates that he is disappointed and will not accept any of them.

Green is making the offer in this case, but the offer is conditional upon his satisfaction with the completed work. Smith can only accept the offer by producing something that meets Green's subjective standards—a risky business. There is no enforceable contract for payments until such time as Green indicates that the completed album is satisfactory.

Suppose Green came to Smith's studio and said that the completed album was satisfactory but then, when Smith delivers it, says it doesn't look right when Green reexamines it at home. That's too late for Green to change his mind. The contract became binding at the moment he indicated that the album was satisfactory. If he then refuses to accept it, he would be breaching his contract.

Earlier I mentioned that contracts for goods worth over $500 must be in writing. Under the Uniform Commercial Code, which governs contracts for the sale of goods, a commission to produce a work is a personal-service contract, as distinct from a contract for the sale of a piece already completed. Therefore, the UCC does not generally apply to commissions.

It is not clear whether the hypothetical situation described above would be considered a contract for the sale of future goods—a wedding album that will be delivered—or whether the agreement would be considered a contract for services the wedding photographer is performing. There is at least one case which suggests that these facts would give rise to a contract for the sale of future goods and be within the coverage of the UCC.

Oral or Written Contracts?

Contracts are enforceable only if they can be proven. The hypothetical examples mentioned above could have been oral contracts, but a great deal of detail is often lost in the course of remembering a conversation. The best practice, of course, is to get it in writing. A written contract not only provides proof, but makes very clear the understanding of both parties regarding the agreement and its terms.

Some people are adamant about doing business strictly on a handshake, particularly where photography is concerned. The assumption seems to be that the best business relations are those based upon mutual trust. And some business people believe that any agreement other than a gentlemen's agreement belies this trust.

Although there may be some validity to these assumptions, people who own small businesses, such as photographers, would nevertheless be well advised to put all of their oral agreements into writing. Far too many people have suffered adverse consequences because of their reliance upon the sanctity of oral contracts.

Even in the best of business relationships, it is still possible that one or both parties might forget the terms of an oral agreement. Or both parties might have quite different perceptions about the precise terms of the agreement reached. When, however, the agreement is put into writing, there is much less doubt as to the terms of the arrangement. Thus a written contract generally functions as a safeguard against subsequent misunderstanding or forgetful minds. In addition, a written contract avoids what is perhaps the principal problem with oral contracts: the fact that they cannot always be proven or enforced.

When Written Contracts Are Necessary

Even if there is no question that an oral contract was made, it may not always be enforceable. There are some agreements which the law requires to be in writing.

An early law that was designed to prevent fraud and perjury, known as the Statute of Frauds, provides that any contract which by its terms cannot be fully performed within one year must be in writing. This rule is narrowly interpreted, so if there is any possibility, no matter how remote, that the contract could be fully performed within one year, the contract need not be reduced to writing.

Assume that a customer and a photographer have entered into a contract in which the photographer has agreed to produce five pictures. Assume further that the agreement requires that the photographer submit one set of proofs per year for five years. In this situation, the terms of the agreement make it impossible for the photographer to complete performance within one year. If, however, the photographer agrees to submit five sets of proofs within a five-year period, it is possible that the photographer could submit all five sets in the first year; therefore, the Statute of Frauds would not apply and the agreement need not be in writing to be enforceable. The fact that the photographer might not actually complete performance within one year is immaterial. So long as complete performance within one year is *possible*, the agreement may be oral.

The Statute of Frauds further provides that certain agreements relating to the sale of goods must be in writing to be enforceable. This provision was codified in the Uniform Sales Act and has now been incorporated into the Uniform Commercial Code. The UCC provides that a contract for the sale of goods costing over $500 is not enforceable unless it is in writing and is signed by the party against whom enforcement is sought. There is no such monetary restriction on service contracts, however. Regardless of the amount of payment, a contract for the sale of services which can be completed within one year need not be in writing.

Distinguishing Sale of Goods from Sale of Services

Obviously, it is important to know whether a particular contract is regarded as involving the sale of goods or the sale of services. The UCC defines goods as being all things that are movable at the time the contract is made, with the exception of the money (or investment securities or certain other types of documents) used as payment for the goods. This definition is sufficiently broad to enable most courts to find that the transactions between a photographer and a supplier of such items as film, paper, cameras, and tripods involve goods. Unfortunately, the distinction is not so clear in the case of agreements between a photographer and a customer.

At least one court has ruled that the photographer-customer contract *is* a contract for the sale of goods, i.e., completed works. In this case, a contract to take wedding pictures was held to be a contract for the sale of goods and thus enforceable.

Determining the Contract Price of Goods

Assuming for the moment that the various agreements entered into by the photographer involve a sale of goods, a second matter to be determined is whether the price of the goods exceeds $500. In most cases, the answer will be clear—but not always.

A photographer, for example, might contract to purchase several camera accessories from a wholesaler. The price for the total purchase exceeds $500, but the price for the individual accessories does not. Which price determines whether or not the statute applies?

Or suppose a photographer sells pictures to a gallery. The gallery will offer the pictures at a price that exceeds $500, but the price the photographer gets is less than $500. Again, which price is used to determine whether the statute applies?

The UCC and the cases interpreting this law provide some guidelines for determining the contract price of goods. The statute provides that the definition of price is to be broadly interpreted to include a payment in money or some other thing of value. The definition of goods in the UCC may be sufficiently broad to include the camera accessories but the problem of the sale of pictures to the gallery remains.

Obviously, a photographer will not in every case be able to ascertain whether the financial terms of a given contract exceed $500, any more than one can always be certain whether a given agreement involves the sale of goods or of services. Given the differences in interpretation by various courts, the best way to ensure that a contract will be enforceable is to put it in clear, unambiguous writing.

No-Cost Written Agreements

At this point, a photographer might claim, with reason, that her profession is taking photographs, not writing legal documents. Where is she going to find the extra time, energy or patience to draft contracts?

Fortunately, you as a photographer will not always need to do this, since the supplier or customers you deal with may be willing to draft satisfactory contracts. However, be wary of someone else's all-purpose contracts—they will almost invariably be one-sided, with all terms drafted in favor of whoever paid to have them prepared.

As a second alternative, you could employ an attorney to draft your contracts. But this may be worthwhile only where the contract involves a substantial transaction. With smaller transactions, the legal fees may be larger than any benefits you'd receive.

The Uniform Commercial Code, a compilation of commercial laws enacted in every state except Louisiana, provides a third and perhaps the best alternative. You need not draft a contract at all or rely on a supplier, customer, or attorney to do so.

The UCC provides that where both parties are merchants and one party sends to the other a written confirmation of an oral contract within a reasonable time after that contract was made, and the recipient does not object to the confirming memorandum within ten days of its receipt, the contract will be deemed enforceable.

A *merchant* is defined as any person who normally deals in goods of the kind sold or who by occupation represents himself as having knowledge or skill peculiar to the practices or goods involved in the transaction. Thus professional photographers and their suppliers will be deemed merchants. Even an amateur photographer will be considered a merchant, since adopting the designation *photographer* would be deemed as representing oneself as having special knowledge or skill in the field. The rule will therefore apply to many oral contracts you might make. Consumers, such as individuals who wish to have a family portrait taken, are probably not merchants within the meaning of the statute.

It should be emphasized that the sole effect of the confirming memorandum is that neither party can use the Statute of Frauds as a defense, assuming that the recipient fails to object within ten days after receipt. The party sending the confirming memorandum must still prove that an oral contract was, in fact, made prior to or at the same time as the written confirmation. But once such proof is offered, neither party can raise the Statute of Frauds to avoid enforcement of the agreement.

The advantage of the confirming memorandum over a written contract is that the confirming memorandum can be used without the active participation of the other contracting party. It would suffice, for example, to simply state:

This memorandum is to confirm our oral agreement.

But since the writer would still have to prove the

terms of that agreement, it would be useful to provide a bit more detail in the confirming memorandum, such as the subject of the contract, the date it was made and the price or other consideration to be paid. Thus you might draft something like the following:

> This memorandum is to confirm our oral agreement made on July 3, 1988, pursuant to which (photographer) agreed to deliver to (magazine editor) on or before September 19, 1988, five photographs for the price of $200.

The advantages of providing some detail to the confirming memorandum are twofold. First, in the event of a dispute, the photographer could introduce the memorandum as proof of the terms of the oral agreement. And second, the recipient of the memorandum will be precluded from offering any proof regarding the terms of the oral contract that contradicts the terms contained in the memorandum. The recipient or, for that matter, the party sending the memorandum, can only introduce proof regarding the terms of the oral contract that are consistent with the terms found in the memorandum. Thus, the editor in the above example would be precluded from claiming that the contract called for delivery of six photographs because the quantity was stated in the memo and not objected to.

On the other hand, the editor would be permitted to testify that the original contract required the photographer to package the pictures in a specific way since this testimony would not contradict the terms stated in the memorandum.

One party to a contract can prevent the other from adding or inventing terms not covered in the confirming memorandum by ending the memo with a clause requiring all other provisions to be contained in a written and signed document. Such a clause might read:

> This is the entire agreement between the
> parties and no modification, alteration,
> or additional terms shall be enforceable
> unless in writing and signed by both
> parties.

To sum up, no one in business should rely on oral contracts alone since they offer little protection in the event of a dispute. The best protection is afforded by a written contract. It is a truism that oral contracts are not worth the paper on which they are written. Where a complete written contract is too burdensome or too costly, the photographer should at least submit a memorandum in confirmation of an oral contract. That at least surpasses the initial barrier raised by the Statute of Frauds. Moreover, by recounting the terms in the memorandum, you, the photographer, will be in a much better position later on to prove the oral contract.

Summary of Essentials to Put in Writing

A contract rarely needs be — or should be — a long, complicated document written in legal jargon designed to provide a handsome income to lawyers. Indeed, a contract should be written in simple language that both parties can understand, and should spell out the terms of the agreement.

The contract would include (1) the date of the agreement; (2) identification of the two parties; (3) a description of the work being sold or, if a service, the service to be performed; (4) the price; and (5) the signatures of the two parties.

To supplement these basics, the agreement should spell out whatever other terms might be applicable: pricing arrangements, payment schedules, copyright ownership, and so forth.

Finally, it should be noted that a written document that leaves out essential terms presents many of the same problems of proof and ambiguity as an oral contract. Contract terms should be well conceived, clearly drafted, "conspicuous" (i.e., not in tiny print that no one can read), and in plain English so everyone understands what the terms are.

Questionable and Broken Contracts

Obviously, you do not want to find yourself involved in contracts of questionable validity, nor do you want to find yourself stuck with a contract that has not been honored. In the first case, how do you spot them; in the second case, what can you do to get justice?

Capacity to Contract

Certain classes of people are deemed by law to lack capacity to contract. The most obvious class is minors, a fact of particular relevance to photographers since a photographer might wish to use a minor as a model. A person is legally a minor until the age of majority, which varies from state to state, but in most cases is either eighteen or twenty-one. A contract entered into by a minor is not necessarily void, but generally is voidable. This means that the minor is free to rescind the contract until reaching the age of majority, but that the other party is bound by the contract if the minor elects to enforce it. In some states a minor over eighteen must restore the consideration (payment) or its equivalent as a condition of rescission. Some states allow a parent to sign on behalf of a minor (see model release forms at the back of the book); other states have a procedure for enabling minors to sign binding nonrescindable contracts. This generally requires the approval of a judge, and since such contracts are highly technical, the photographer who wishes to make one would be well advised to consult a lawyer.

Illegal Contracts

If either the consideration (which is normally money) or the subject matter of the contract is illegal, the contract itself is illegal. This problem will not normally arise in photography contracts, but it is possible that a photographer could unwittingly become a party to an illegal contract. For example, the state of New York has enacted a statute, popularly known as the Son of Sam Law, that prohibits criminals from receiving financial compensation from the exploitation and commercialization of their crimes. Such statutes are being increasingly adopted. Presently, the federal government and the vast majority of states have Son of Sam laws. A publisher who contracts to pay a criminal royalties in return for the criminal's story would be violating the statute, and the contract would therefore be illegal. The same would probably be true of an agreement made by a photographer to illustrate a criminal's story in exchange for some payment. It is not certain, however, whether someone could circumvent the statute by paying a criminal for other services. Life magazine paid $9,000 to Bernard Welch, convicted murderer of Michael Halberstam, for the exclusive rights to photographs from the Welch family album. It remains to be seen whether such pictures would fall within the scope of a Son of Sam type of statute.

A photographer may also become a party to an illegal contract if the work resulting from that contract is found to be either obscene or libelous. (Obscenity is discussed in Chapter 4 and libel, in Chapter 2.)

Generally, a photographer is not liable for a deceptive or fraudulent use of his work unless he knew his work would be used in a dishonest manner. Even so, a photographer should always try to guard against potential fraud claims by avoiding participation in a deception. As a general rule, if the subject matter to be photographed is obviously misleading, beware.

The Federal Trade Commission is responsible for preventing "unfair methods of competition in commerce and unfair or deceptive acts or practices in commerce." This act also explicitly makes persons, partnerships, and corporations liable for deceptive advertising. The FTC has the authority to issue orders requiring corrective advertising.

There is no hard and fast rule for determining what constitutes an unfair or deceptive act or practice. As for deceptive advertising, the phrase means an advertisement that is materially misleading. An advertisement is deceptive if it has the "tendency" or "capacity" to deceive the public. The Commission may examine an advertisement and determine its potential effect on the minds of consumers without considering public opinion or even hearing evidence by complaining parties. The Commission may even find an advertisement violates the FTC Act despite consumers' testimony that they would not be misled by it. For instance, the truth in advertising law provides that a photographer will be liable for any deception in shooting an advertisement. General Foods has issued a policy statement regarding food photography which provides useful guidelines for any photographer.

- Food will be photographed in an unadulterated states—the product must be typical of that normally packed; with no preselection for quality or substitution of individual components.

- Individual portions must conform to amount per serving used in describing yield.

- Package amounts shown must conform to package yield.

- The product must be prepared according to package directions.

- A recipe must follow directions and be shown in the same condition it would appear in when suitable for serving.

- Mock-ups may not be used.

- Props should be typical of those readily available to the consumers.

- Theatrical devices (unusual camera angles, small-size bowls and spoons) may not be used to make false implications.

The law generally treats an illegal contract as *void* rather than merely *voidable*—an important distinction. A voidable contract is valid until it is voided by the party possessing the right to rescind, whereas a void contract is not binding on either party, and neither party will be permitted to enjoy any fruits of the agreement. A void contract results when both parties are at fault or where the illegality involves a morally reprehensible crime. If, however, the illegality involves an act which is wrong only because the law says that it is (as, for example, illegal parking or not obtaining a necessary business license), one party may have some rights against the less innocent party. A photographer who anticipates entering into, or is already involved in, a contract of questionable legality would be well advised to consult a lawyer.

Unconscionable Contracts

The law generally gives the parties involved in a contract complete freedom to contract. Thus, contractual terms which are unfair, unjust, or even ludicrous will generally be enforced if they are legal. But this freedom is not without limits; the parties are not free to make a contract which is unconscionable. *Unconscionability* is an elusive concept, but the courts have certain guidelines in ruling on it. A given contract is likely to be considered unconscionable if it is grossly unfair and the parties lack equal bargaining power. Photographers who are just starting out are typically in a weaker bargaining position than advertising clients or owners of stock photo businesses and are therefore more likely to win a suit on an allegation of unconscionability. This is especially true where the photographer has simply signed a magazine's form contract. If the form contract is extremely one-sided in favor of the magazine, and if the photographer was given the choice of signing the contract unchanged or not contracting at all, a court could find that the agreement was unconscionable. If that happens, the court may either treat the contract as void or strike the unconscionable clauses and enforce the remainder. It should be noted that unconscionability is generally used as a defense by the one who is sued for breach of contract, and that the defense is rarely successful, particularly where both parties are business people.

WHAT HAPPENS WHEN A CONTRACT IS BROKEN?

Specific Performance

The principle underlying all remedies for breach of contract is to satisfy the wronged party's expectations: that is, the courts will attempt to place the injured party in the position that would have resulted had the contract been fully performed. Courts and the legislatures have devised a number of remedies to provide aggrieved parties with the benefit of their bargains. Generally, this will take the form of monetary damages, but where monetary damages fail to solve the problem, the court may order *specific performance*. Specific performance means the breaching party is ordered to perform as promised. This remedy is generally reserved for cases in which the contract involves unique goods. In photography, a court might specifically enforce a contract to produce wedding pictures by compelling the photographer to deliver the photographs to the customer, but only if the photographs had been printed, qualifying as goods. A court would not be likely to compel a photographer to shoot or develop prints (thus performing a service) as a means of satisfying the aggrieved customer. The Thirteenth Amendment of the Constitution prohibits one from being forced to perform labor against one's will. Thus, for breach of a personal-service contract, monetary damages are generally awarded.

Photos Kept Too Long

Frequently, photographers or photo agencies will submit prints or transparencies to a potential purchaser on approval. If this submission is the result of an oral agreement, i.e., the photos were requested, the customer may be liable for holding fees if the photographs are kept for an unreasonable time without payment.

Ordinarily, the delivery memos that accompany requested photographs contain clauses specifying that the customer is liable for any loss or damage to the photographs. A delivery memo may contain provisions that specify a certain amount the customer must pay for each lost or damaged picture. These provisions are enforceable if the amount they specify is a reasonable estimate of the value of the photos and not a penalty. Delivery memos are designed to be signed and returned by the customer; however, they are usually effective and enforceable even if not signed.

Damages against Loss of Film or Photographs

The law allows recovery of damages against film processors who lose or damage film, or, in some cases, who lose or damage photographs. However, recovery may be limited to the cost of the film alone. In *Goor v. Navillo* the plaintiff's vacation pictures were lost by the photo lab to which he entrusted them for processing. The film carton had the following disclaimer: "The film in this carton has been made with great care and will be processed in our laboratory without additional charge. If we find the film to have been defective in manufacture or to have been damaged in our laboratory, we will replace it, but we assume no other responsibility either express or implied." The court held that recovery was limited to the replacement cost of the film because of the written disclaimer.

In *Willard Van Dyke Productions v. Eastman Kodak* the facts are similar to those in *Goor* except that the film carton stated that the processing was not included in the price of the film; therefore, the court allowed full recovery of lost profits.

In *Mieske v. Bartell Drug Co.* the plaintiff was a home photographer who sued a drugstore for losing the plaintiff's thirty-two reels of home movie film. Although the drugstore gave the plaintiff a receipt that included a clause disclaiming liability beyond the retail cost of the film, the court found the disclaimer invalid and unconscionable. The court reasoned that Article 2 of the Uniform Commercial Code, which provides that unconscionable disclaimers will not be upheld, applies to bailments as well as to the sale of goods.* The court noted that such disclaimers should not be upheld between a commercial film processor and a retail customer because retail customers probably do not notice or understand a disclaimer clause on a receipt. However, such a disclaimer might be valid among people within the photography industry—people who would be expected to know about and understand the disclaimer.

Concerning the *amount* of recovery, the cases all show that the photographer can always recover at least the cost of the damaged film. In addition, the photographer can often recover the value of the photographs that would have resulted had the film been processed properly.

There are various ways in which courts determine the damages a photographer receives in such cases. As a first step, the court will attempt to calculate the market value of photographs that would have been made from the lost or damaged film. Market value is determined by the prior use made of the photograph, the current price for use of such photographs, and the extent to which the photograph has already been used. For example, an old (though not an antique) transparency or negative might have less value than a newer one because its useful life as a commercial photograph is shorter. On the other hand, it might have historical importance. Also, certain subjects are more commercially valuable or salable than others.

Finally, courts consider the ease with which certain pictures may be retaken.

Sometimes the market value of film or pictures is hard to ascertain. In such cases, courts have uniformly held that a variety of factors may be used to determine the value of the film or photographs. In *Dr. Carlton Ray v. The American Museum of Natural History*, a well-known scientist/photographer delivered to the Museum of Natural History original color transparencies of indigenous species he took in the Antarctic. The museum failed to return eleven of the transparencies. Dr. Ray attempted to establish the cost of replacement or reproduction of the transparencies, based upon either the actual cash outlay or the value of the required labor and materials. In his testimony Ray told the court that the location where the transparencies were taken was remote; the transparencies were taken underwater, which was extremely hazardous; they were the best of the shots he took; and they had "data value," i.e., it was impossible to reproduce the conditions under which the pictures were taken.

The court determined that the fair and reasonable value of the transparencies was $15,000 because if there is a total loss of property with no ascertainable market value, the measure of damages is the cost to replace or reproduce the article and if it cannot be reproduced or replaced, then its actual value to the owner should be considered in fixing damages.

In other words, it has been found that just because the value was speculative, uncertain, even difficult to prove, there was no ground for denying recovery or for limiting such recovery to nominal damages only.

In one case, photographer Brian Wolff realized the importance of having his paperwork in order. When *Geo* magazine had 76 of his photos stolen from it, it became necessary to identify each chrome and place a value on it. Fortunately, the photographer's tear sheets contained this essential information. In the *Don Johnson v. Nike* case, one issue was the value of the photographer's lost slides. Experts in the industry testified that $1500 per transparency was reasonable given Johnson's status, the sales price for his other works and the fact that some of the photos were irreplaceable. Fifteen hundred dollars appears to be the standard price for a lost slide by a professional photographer, yet some works have been valued even higher. For example, John G. Zimmerman received $3,000.00 per slide in 1988, when he was able to

---

*Bailment is the rightful temporary possession of someone else's property; parking a car in a parking lot, for example, establishes a bailment, as does leaving film with a processor.

establish the exceptional and irreplaceable nature of his action-oriented slides spanning a 40-year period. Similarly, photographer John Stevens recovered over $22,000.00 for a lost slide of Salvador Dali.

Photographer Ethan Hoffman won a substantial judgment against Portogallo, Inc., when the lab lost ten rolls of film which were part of a larger series. The court awarded the photographer $1,500 per lost image for a total of $486,000 ($632,586 with interest added) based on the uniqueness of the subject matter, Hoffman's status as a prestigious photojournalist and the number of times his work had been published. In addition, Hoffman had commitments from two major magazines to publish some of the lost pictures. Unfortunately, the judgment may be uncollectable since the lab promptly ceased doing business.

Photographers should also be aware of the fact that mail services usually have specific liability limitations for lost or damaged goods. These limitations vary from carrier to carrier and should be checked prior to mailing any work. If additional coverage is desired, it can usually be purchased through the carrier or from the photographer's own insurer. In one case, *Lieberman v. Airborne Freight Corp.*, the federal district judge in New York indicated that the commercial sophistication and knowledge of the photographer was a critical issue when determining the carrier's liability. In this case, however, the photographer had not been given the air bill which contained the limitations of liability.

Chapter 10

DEALING WITH AGENTS

Many photographers are successful in selling their own work, either directly to clients or to intermediaries such as galleries. Other photographers are employed on a regular basis—for example as staff photographers for newspapers. A third group of photographers are independent and depend on stock agencies to make their work available to the largest possible number of potential buyers. A very small number of photographers—the handful who have reached the top of their profession—employ the services of personal photographic agents to assist in obtaining commissions or in selling existing work.

Stock agents keep files of photographs classified by subject. Ordinarily, they sell the use of a photograph for one time by the buyer—this arrangement is analogous to a rental. Usually, stock agents keep between 40 and 60 percent of the proceeds of a sale, although 50 percent is very common. Many photographers prefer to place different copies of their work with more than one stock agent (assuming they have non-exclusive agency agreements). One way a photographer can accomplish the multiple placement is by taking several shots of important subjects. In the past this could also be done by making duplicate slides, but that practice is being discouraged now because of the risk of different agencies selling the one-time use of what is believed to be a unique image and turns out not to be. Enough legal problems have resulted from the use of duplicate slides to cause agencies to advise photographers to shoot slightly different views of important subjects when making use of more than one stock agency—and to avoid making duplicate slides. Some stock agents request that photographers type captions and affix them to the mounts of transparencies and include the letters MRA, which mean Model Release Available. Stock houses have different requirements as to film and paper and size of transparency.

Stock agencies are responsible for works while they are in the agency's possession. It is for this reason that most of them require individuals who remove transparencies from the agencies to sign for them. In one case, an advertising agency was held liable for $94,500.00 plus costs and attorney's fees when it lost 63 transparencies that it had borrowed. The stock agency, National Stock Network, used an ASMP form which contained a provision stating that the parties agreed that the value of each transparency would be $1,500.00. The form also required all disputes to be submitted to binding arbitration. For this reason, proceeding was resolved more expeditiously than it would have been if it had been handled in the traditional manner by a judge and jury.

A directory of national and international stock agencies entitled "The Photo Marketing Handbook" is available from Images Press, 22 East 17th St., New York, New York 10003 at $18.95 postpaid.

The *personal photographic agent*, also known as a rep, usually handles all the work of a few clients. He knows buyers and usually makes the initial contact with them on behalf of the photographer. He may obtain assignments and do billing and promotion and may act as a business manager and marketer. One way to find a personal photographic agent is to write to SPAR (Society of Photographers and Artists Representatives), P.O. Box 845, FDR Station, New York, NY 10150. SPAR sells a list that outlines its members' specialties and clients. Photographic representatives usually charge a 25 percent commission.

The Personal Agent As Contract Negotiator

A personal photographic agent performs a wide variety of services, but when acting as matchmaker between a photographer and a client, the agent must be sensitive to the needs of both parties. If those needs are in conflict, the agent will have to act as a negotiator. This intermediary role is never more important than in contractual matters.

If a client is interested in commissioning a work,

the process of negotiating a photographer-client contract begins. The institutional client generally may offer the photographer a form or standard contract, but such a contract is rarely accepted in its entirety. Rather, a series of offers and counteroffers will ensue until mutually satisfactory terms have been agreed upon, or until it becomes apparent that an agreement cannot be reached. Non-institutional customers may not have forms; therefore the photographer or agent may have to provide the draft contract.

The agent's role in contract negotiations will normally be to attempt to get the best contract possible for the photographer without unduly antagonizing the customer. Most clients are glad to negotiate with an agent, because agents familiar with the legal and trade terminology and practices tend to facilitate the process. Moreover, since agents are constantly involved in negotiations between various photographers and clients, they are usually in the best position to identify an acceptable contract, and can be trusted to moderate unreasonable or unrealistic demands made by either party.

Suggested Precautions

To protect against possible liability, a photographer should choose an experienced, legitimate agency or agent and clearly delineate the scope of that party's authority in a well-drafted agency agreement checked over by a lawyer familiar with photography law. Most established agencies have their own form contracts, so your attorney should assist you in evaluating the acceptability of the agency's contract. If you will be using the services of a personal photographic agent, you should take care to define the scope of the agent's authority.

Chapter 11

HOW TO FIND A LAWYER

Most photographers expect to seek the advice of a lawyer only occasionally, for counseling on important matters such as potential defamation or invasion of privacy liability. If you are a serious photographer, you should establish an early relationship with an attorney. An attorney experienced in publishing or art law should also be able to give you important information regarding areas of liability exposure unique to your work, such as portrayal of someone in a false light, invasion of privacy, pornography and obscenity, libel, copyright infringement, breach of the photographer-customer contract, etc.

If employees assist you in shooting and developing, you should also have advice on your legal relationship with present and future employees. Ignorance of these issues can lead to inadvertent violation of the rules, which in turn can result in financially devastating lawsuits and even criminal penalties. Each state has its own laws covering certain business practices; thus, state laws must be consulted on many areas in this book. A competent local business attorney is, therefore, your best source of information on many issues which will arise in the running of your business.

What is really behind all the hoopla about "preventive legal counseling"? Are we lawyers simply seeking more work? Admittedly, as business people, lawyers want business. But what you should consider is economic reality: *Most legal problems cost more to solve or defend than it would have cost to prevent them in the first place.* Litigation is notoriously inefficient and expensive. You do not want to sue or to be sued, if you can help it. The expense is shocking; for instance, it can cost close to one hundred dollars per day simply to use a courtroom for trial. Pretrial procedures run into the thousands of dollars on most cases. The cost of defending a case filed against you is something you have no choice about, unless you choose to default, which is almost never advisable.

One of the first items you should discuss with your lawyer is the fee structure. You are entitled to an estimate, though unless you enter into an agreement to the contrary with the attorney, the estimate is just that. Business and publishing lawyers generally charge by the hour, though you may be quoted a flat rate for a specific service such as incorporation or review of a contract.

If you do not know any attorneys, ask other photographers and publishers whether they know any good ones. You want a lawyer who specializes in copyright and/or publishing law. Finding the lawyer who is right for you is like finding the right doctor; you may have to shop around a bit. Your city, county, and state bar associations may have helpful referral services. A good tip is to find out who is in the intellectual property section of the state or county bar association, or who has served on special bar committees dealing with intellectual property law. It may also be useful to find out whether any articles covering the area of law you are concerned with have been published in either scholarly journals or continuing legal-education publications, and if the author is available to assist you. Your state or county law librarian can assist you here.

It is a good idea to hire a specialist or law firm with a number of specialists rather than a general practitioner. While you may pay more per hour for the expert, you will not be funding his learning time. The specialist's experience will be worth the higher hourly rate.

One aid in finding a lawyer who represents photographers is the *Martindale-Hubbell Law Directory*, which can be found in your local county law library. (However, not all lawyers are listed in the directory. The mere fact that a particular attorney's name does not appear in the book should not give you cause for concern, since there is a charge for being included and some lawyers choose not to pay for the listing.)

After you have obtained some names, it would be appropriate for you to talk with several attorneys for a short period of time to evaluate them. Do not be afraid to ask about their background and experience, and whether they feel they can help you.

Once you have completed the interview process, select the lawyer with whom you are most comfortable. The rest is up to you. Contact your attorney whenever you believe you have a legal question.

I encourage my clients to feel comfortable about calling me at the office during the day or at home in the evening. Some lawyers, however, may resent having their personal time invaded. Some, in fact, do not list their home telephone numbers. Learn your attorney's preference early on.

You should feel comfortable when confiding in your attorney and feel that whatever information you pass on will be held in confidence. Disclosure of your confidential communications, under most circumstances, would be considered an ethical breach which could subject your lawyer to professional sanctions.

If you develop a good relationship with the right attorney, you may find that your increased confidence in understanding your legal situations actually increases your effectiveness as a photographer.

Chapter 12

FORMS AND SAMPLE CONTRACTS

What Are Photographs Worth?

Obviously, it is impossible to suggest what a photograph is worth in exact terms. What follows is a practical compilation of prices that a major stock agency suggests for usage fees. These are current as this book goes to press in 1989. As this agency (Superstock International Inc.) advises, because of the many variances, it is difficult to pinpoint all usage possibilities. In general, the prices are based on exposure of the photograph. This includes the size (full page or fraction) and positioning (cover or inside), and the print run or circulation. Unless specified, U.S. rights are for one year

We thank Superstock International Inc. for their permission to reprint the following pricing information.

Corporate & Collateral

Annual Reports Company Booklets

Print Run	Inside*	Cover**
Under 10K	$350 – 500	800
10 – 30K	450 – 600	1,000
30 – 100K	550 – 750	1,200

Variables: *Spreads, add 50%; **Rate for single photo. Multiple photos on cover, call for quote

Brochures Catalogs, Sales, Product Spec Sheets, Flyers, Recruitment, Rack Folders

Print Run	Inside*	Cover**
Under 10K	275 – 425	650
10 – 30K	300 – 450	750
30 – 100K	400 – 650	950
100 – 500K	500 – 900	1,250

Variables: *Spreads, add 50%; **Rate for single photo. Multiple photos on cover, call for quote; Rack folders, less 20%

Audio Visual Industrial, Trade Shows, Etc.

Photos per Show	1–3 Showings
1 – 5	150 each
6 – 10	125 each
11 – 20	100 each
21 – 50	75 each

Variables: Add 10% for 4–12 showings; add 25% for unlimited one year use

Packaging Three year exclusive use

Distribution	Size of Photo
Local	450 – 1,200
Regional	600 – 2,400
National	750 – 3,500

Variables: Test runs – 50% of full rate; re-use – 75% of full rate

Direct Advertising

Point Of Purchase

Print Run	Rate based on size of image
Under 10K	$ 500 – 950
10K – 30K	900 – 1,500
30K – 100K	1,200 – 2,000

Rights are for one year, rate based on one photo

Billboards

Locations	Rate based on size of image and market
1 – 12	500 – 1,000
13 – 50	1,000 – 1,800
50 – 100	1,800 – 2,500

Rights are up to one year, rate based on one photo

Transit Displays Car Cards, Bus Cards, Terminals, Etc.

Exposure	3 Mos. – 1 Year
Under 2,000 Units	600 – 1,000
2,000 to 10,000 Units	800 – 2,000

Variables: 30-50% Surcharge for major, high density terminal locations; rights are for one year, rate based on one photo

Exhibit Displays Trade Shows, Retail Displays, Etc.

Duration	Rate based on size of image
Up to one week	400 – 500
Up to one year	600 – 1,200

Variables: Displays for lobbies, offices, etc., see Wall Decor.

Editorial

Textbooks & Tradebooks

Print Run	1/4 pg	1/2 pg	3/4 pg	Full pg	Cover
Under 40K	$175	200	250	300	600
40 – 100K	200	225	275	325	800

Variables: Double page, add 80%; Unit or Chapter Openers, Frontispiece, etc: add 25%; Revisions: 75% of current fee

Rights: Rates are for one time U.S. English Language Rights
One Time World Rights, one language, add 100%;
One Time Rights each additional language, add 25%;
One Time Rights for 5 additional languages, add 100%;
One Time World Rights – all languages, add 200%

Encyclopedia

Print Run	1/4 pg	1/2 pg	3/4 pg	Full pg	Cover
Under 40K	210	250	275	300	750
40 – 100K	235	275	300	325	1,000

Magazines

Circulation	1/4 pg	1/2 pg	3/4 pg	Full pg	Cover
Up to 100K	150	200	250	300	700
100 – 500K	200	250	300	350	850
500K – 1M	250	300	350	400	1,200
1 – 3M	350	400	450	550	1,500

Variables: Double page, add 80%;
House Organs: Magazine rate less 20%;
Advertorial: add 80%

Newspapers

Circulation	1/4 page	1/2 page	Full page
Under 100K	150	200	400
100 – 250K	200	250	500
Over 250K	250	350	700

Variables: Sunday Supplement, add 25%

Television

Editorial use	Each photo
Local	175
Regional	200
National	250

Variable: Multiple use, price upon request

Media Advertising

Consumer Magazines (One Photo, 1–3 Insertions)

Circulation	Rate based on size of photo and circulation
100K – 1 Million	$ 650 – 1,400
1 Million – 4 Million	1,200 – 2,200

Variables: Additional photos–same Ad: 2 to 4, add 50% each; 5 to 10, add 25% each; Add'l insertions: 4 to 9, add 30%, 10 to 20, add 60%;
Double page spread: add 40%; B&W Usage: Less 10%;
Retail, Travel and Real Estate: Less 10%;
Unlimited 1 Year: add 100%;
Advertorial: add 80% to editorial rate

Trade Magazines (One Photo, 1–3 Insertions)

Circulation	Rate based on size of photo and circulation
Less than 80K	500 – 800
80K to 200K	750 – 1,200
200K to 500K	1,000 – 1,600

Variables: See Consumer Magazines above

Newspapers (One Photo, 1–3 Insertions)

	Rate based on size of photo and market size
Local	300 – 550
Regional	500 – 750
National	700 – 1,200

Variables: See Consumer Magazines above

Television

	One photo for 13 week cycle commercial; rates determined by size of market
Local	250 – 400
Regional	350 – 500
National	750

Variables: Additional cycles: add 50% each;
One year unlimited: 100%;
Additional photo per commercial, add 50% each

Miscellaneous

Calendars

Retail Calendars	Rate based on print run and duration of exclusivity
U.S. Rights	$350 – 650

Variables: Single hanger, add 50%;
World Rights,
Advertising calendars, call for prices

Posters

U.S. Rights	Rate based on size, print run and duration
Promotional	400 – 900
Retail	350 – 600
Educational & Study Print	300 – 500

Variables: Fees based on royalties available, call to discuss

Greeting Cards

	Rate based on print run and duration
U.S. Rights	300 – 500

Puzzles

	Rate based on print run
U.S. Rights	350 – 650

Tape & Record Albums Compact Disc

	Rate based on print run
Front Cover	400 – 600
Back Cover	300 – 400
Cover Wrap	600 – 900
Enclosures	200 – 300
Test Only	250 – 350

Variables: Add 50% for both album, tape and/or CD—when purchased together

Postcards (Retail) $200 for up to 20K print run

Wall Decor from $200, call for quote

Comp Fee $100 each (deductible)

Artist Rendering 75% of repro fee
Artist Reference: 1 – 3 photos, $150 each.

Non-Profit 15% less

FORM VA
UNITED STATES COPYRIGHT OFFICE

REGISTRATION NUMBER

VA   VAU

EFFECTIVE DATE OF REGISTRATION

_____
Month   Day   Year

DO NOT WRITE ABOVE THIS LINE. IF YOU NEED MORE SPACE, USE A SEPARATE CONTINUATION SHEET.

1

TITLE OF THIS WORK ▼   **NATURE OF THIS WORK ▼** See instructions

PREVIOUS OR ALTERNATIVE TITLES ▼

PUBLICATION AS A CONTRIBUTION If this work was published as a contribution to a periodical, serial, or collection, give information about the collective work in which the contribution appeared. **Title of Collective Work ▼**

If published in a periodical or serial give: **Volume ▼**   **Number ▼**   **Issue Date ▼**   **On Pages ▼**

2

NOTE

Under the law, the "author" of a "work made for hire" is generally the employer, not the employee (see instructions). For any part of this work that was "made for hire" check "Yes" in the space provided, give the employer (or other person for whom the work was prepared) as "Author" of that part, and leave the space for dates of birth and death blank.

a

NAME OF AUTHOR ▼   **DATES OF BIRTH AND DEATH**
Year Born ▼   Year Died ▼

Was this contribution to the work a "work made for hire"?
☐ Yes
☐ No

AUTHOR'S NATIONALITY OR DOMICILE
Name of Country
OR { Citizen of ▶_____
Domiciled in ▶_____

WAS THIS AUTHOR'S CONTRIBUTION TO THE WORK
Anonymous?   ☐ Yes ☐ No
Pseudonymous?   ☐ Yes ☐ No
If the answer to either of these questions is "Yes," see detailed instructions.

NATURE OF AUTHORSHIP Briefly describe nature of the material created by this author in which copyright is claimed. ▼

b

NAME OF AUTHOR ▼   **DATES OF BIRTH AND DEATH**
Year Born ▼   Year Died ▼

Was this contribution to the work a "work made for hire"?
☐ Yes
☐ No

AUTHOR'S NATIONALITY OR DOMICILE
Name of country
OR { Citizen of ▶_____
Domiciled in ▶_____

WAS THIS AUTHOR'S CONTRIBUTION TO THE WORK
Anonymous?   ☐ Yes ☐ No
Pseudonymous?   ☐ Yes ☐ No
If the answer to either of these questions is "Yes," see detailed instructions.

NATURE OF AUTHORSHIP Briefly describe nature of the material created by this author in which copyright is claimed. ▼

c

NAME OF AUTHOR ▼   **DATES OF BIRTH AND DEATH**
Year Born ▼   Year Died ▼

Was this contribution to the work a "work made for hire"?
☐ Yes
☐ No

AUTHOR'S NATIONALITY OR DOMICILE
Name of Country
OR { Citizen of ▶_____
Domiciled in ▶_____

WAS THIS AUTHOR'S CONTRIBUTION TO THE WORK
Anonymous?   ☐ Yes ☐ No
Pseudonymous?   ☐ Yes ☐ No
If the answer to either of these questions is "Yes," see detailed instructions.

NATURE OF AUTHORSHIP Briefly describe nature of the material created by this author in which copyright is claimed. ▼

3

YEAR IN WHICH CREATION OF THIS WORK WAS COMPLETED This information must be given in all cases.
◀ Year

DATE AND NATION OF FIRST PUBLICATION OF THIS PARTICULAR WORK
Complete this information ONLY if this work has been published.
Month ▶ _____ Day ▶ _____ Year ▶ _____   ◀ Nation

4

See instructions before completing this space.

COPYRIGHT CLAIMANT(S) Name and address must be given even if the claimant is the same as the author given in space 2.▼

TRANSFER If the claimant(s) named here in space 4 are different from the author(s) named in space 2, give a brief statement of how the claimant(s) obtained ownership of the copyright.▼

DO NOT WRITE HERE OFFICE USE ONLY
APPLICATION RECEIVED
ONE DEPOSIT RECEIVED
TWO DEPOSITS RECEIVED
REMITTANCE NUMBER AND DATE

MORE ON BACK ▶ • Complete all applicable spaces (numbers 5-9) on the reverse side of this page.
• See detailed instructions.   • Sign the form at line 8.

DO NOT WRITE HERE
Page 1 of_____pages

EXAMINED BY _____

FORM VA

CHECKED BY _____

☐ CORRESPONDENCE Yes

☐ DEPOSIT ACCOUNT FUNDS USED

FOR COPYRIGHT OFFICE USE ONLY

DO NOT WRITE ABOVE THIS LINE. IF YOU NEED MORE SPACE, USE A SEPARATE CONTINUATION SHEET.

PREVIOUS REGISTRATION Has registration for this work, or for an earlier version of this work, already been made in the Copyright Office?

☐ Yes ☐ No If your answer is "Yes," why is another registration being sought? (Check appropriate box) ▼

☐ This is the first published edition of a work previously registered in unpublished form.

☐ This is the first application submitted by this author as copyright claimant.

☐ This is a changed version of the work, as shown by space 6 on this application.

If your answer is "Yes," give: **Previous Registration Number** ▼   **Year of Registration** ▼

5

DERIVATIVE WORK OR COMPILATION Complete both space 6a & 6b for a derivative work; complete only 6b for a compilation.

a. Preexisting Material Identify any preexisting work or works that this work is based on or incorporates. ▼

_____

_____

b. Material Added to This Work Give a brief, general statement of the material that has been added to this work and in which copyright is claimed.▼

_____

_____

6

See instructions before completing this space.

DEPOSIT ACCOUNT If the registration fee is to be charged to a Deposit Account established in the Copyright Office, give name and number of Account.

Name ▼   **Account Number** ▼

7

CORRESPONDENCE Give name and address to which correspondence about this application should be sent. Name/Address/Apt/City/State/Zip ▼

_____

_____

Area Code & Telephone Number ▶

Be sure to give your daytime phone ◀ number.

CERTIFICATION* I, the undersigned, hereby certify that I am the

Check only one ▼

☐ author

☐ other copyright claimant

☐ owner of exclusive right(s)

☐ authorized agent of _____
Name of author or other copyright claimant, or owner of exclusive right(s) ▲

8

of the work identified in this application and that the statements made
by me in this application are correct to the best of my knowledge.

Typed or printed name and date ▼ If this is a published work, this date must be the same as or later than the date of publication given in space 3.

_____   date ▶ _____

👉 Handwritten signature (X) ▼

MAIL CERTIFICATE TO

Name ▼

Number/Street/Apartment Number ▼

City/State/ZIP ▼

Certificate will be mailed in window envelope

Have you:
- Completed all necessary spaces?
- Signed your application in space 8?
- Enclosed check or money order for $10 payable to *Register of Copyrights?*
- Enclosed your deposit material with the application and fee?

MAIL TO: Register of Copyrights, Library of Congress, Washington, D.C. 20559.

9

* 17 U.S.C. § 506(e): Any person who knowingly makes a false representation of a material fact in the application for copyright registration provided for by section 409, or in any written statement filed in connection with the application, shall be fined not more than $2,500.

☆U.S. GOVERNMENT PRINTING OFFICE: 1988—241-428/80,010   November 1988—25,000

Filling Out Application Form VA

Detach and read these instructions before completing this form. Make sure all applicable spaces have been filled in before you return this form.

BASIC INFORMATION

When to Use This Form: Use Form VA for copyright registration of published or unpublished works of the visual arts. This category consists of "pictorial, graphic, or sculptural works," including two-dimensional and three-dimensional works of fine, graphic, and applied art, photographs, prints and art reproductions, maps, globes, charts, technical drawings, diagrams, and models.

What Does Copyright Protect? Copyright in a work of the visual arts protects those pictorial, graphic, or sculptural elements that, either alone or in combination, represent an "original work of authorship." The statute declares: "In no case does copyright protection for an original work of authorship extend to any idea, procedure, process, system, method of operation, concept, principle, or discovery, regardless of the form in which it is described, explained, illustrated, or embodied in such work."

Works of Artistic Craftsmanship and Designs: "Works of artistic craftsmanship" are registrable on Form VA, but the statute makes clear that protection extends to "their form" and not to "their mechanical or utilitarian aspects." The "design of a useful article" is considered copyrightable "only if, and only to the extent that, such design incorporates pictorial, graphic, or sculptural features that can be identified separately from, and are capable of existing independently of, the utilitarian aspects of the article."

Labels and Advertisements: Works prepared for use in connection with the sale or advertisement of goods and services are registrable if they contain "original work of authorship." Use Form VA if the copyrightable material in the work you are registering is mainly pictorial or graphic; use Form TX if it consists mainly of text. **NOTE:** Words and short phrases such as names, titles, and slogans cannot be protected by copyright, and the same is true of standard symbols, emblems, and other commonly used graphic designs that are in the public domain. When used commercially, material of that sort can sometimes be protected under state laws of unfair competition or under the Federal trademark laws. For information about trademark registration, write to the Commissioner of Patents and Trademarks, Washington, D.C. 20231.

Deposit to Accompany Application: An application for copyright registration must be accompanied by a deposit consisting of copies representing the en-tire work for which registration is to be made.

Unpublished Work: Deposit one complete copy.

Published Work: Deposit two complete copies of the best edition.

Work First Published Outside the United States: Deposit one complete copy of the first foreign edition.

Contribution to a Collective Work: Deposit one complete copy of the best edition of the collective work.

The Copyright Notice: For published works, the law provides that a copyright notice in a specified form "shall be placed on all publicly distributed copies from which the work can be visually perceived." Use of the copyright notice is the responsibility of the copyright owner and does not require advance permission from the Copyright Office. The required form of the notice for copies generally consists of three elements: (1) the symbol "©", or the word "Copyright," or the abbreviation "Copr."; (2) the year of first publication; and (3) the name of the owner of copyright. For example: "© 1981 Constance Porter." The notice is to be affixed to the copies "in such manner and location as to give reasonable notice of the claim of copyright."

For further information about copyright registration, notice, or special questions relating to copyright problems, write:

Information and Publications Section, LM-455
Copyright Office, Library of Congress, Washington, D.C. 20559

LINE-BY-LINE INSTRUCTIONS

1 SPACE 1: Title

Title of This Work: Every work submitted for copyright registration must be given a title to identify that particular work. If the copies of the work bear a title (or an identifying phrase that could serve as a title), transcribe that wording *completely* and *exactly* on the application. Indexing of the registration and future identification of the work will depend on the information you give here.

Previous or Alternative Titles: Complete this space if there are any additional titles for the work under which someone searching for the registration might be likely to look, or under which a document pertaining to the work might be recorded.

Publication as a Contribution: If the work being registered is a contribution to a periodical, serial, or collection, give the title of the contribution in the "Title of This Work" space. Then, in the line headed "Publication as a Contribution," give information about the collective work in which the contribution appeared.

Nature of This Work: Briefly describe the general nature or character of the pictorial, graphic, or sculptural work being registered for copyright. Examples: "Oil Painting"; "Charcoal Drawing"; "Etching"; "Sculpture"; "Map"; "Photograph"; "Scale Model"; "Lithographic Print"; "Jewelry Design"; "Fabric Design."

2 SPACE 2: Author(s)

General Instructions: After reading these instructions, decide who are the "authors" of this work for copyright purposes. Then, unless the work is a "collective work," give the requested information about every "author" who contributed any appreciable amount of copyrightable matter to this version of the work. If you need further space, request additional Continuation Sheets. In the case of a collective work, such as a catalog of paintings or collection of cartoons by various authors, give information about the author of the collec-tive work as a whole.

Name of Author: The fullest form of the author's name should be given. Unless the work was "made for hire," the individual who actually created the work is its "author." In the case of a work made for hire, the statute provides that "the employer or other person for whom the work was prepared is considered the author."

What is a "Work Made for Hire"? A "work made for hire" is defined as: (1) "a work prepared by an employee within the scope of his or her employment"; or (2) "a work specially ordered or commissioned for use as a contribution to a collective work, as a part of a motion picture or other audiovisual work, as a translation, as a supplementary work, as a compilation, as an instructional text, as a test, as answer material for a test, or as an atlas, if the parties expressly agree in a written instrument signed by them that the work shall be considered a work made for hire." If you have checked "Yes" to indicate that the work was "made for hire," you must give the full legal name of the employer (or other person for whom the work was prepared). You may also include the name of the employee along with the name of the employer (for example: "Elster Publishing Co., employer for hire of John Ferguson").

"Anonymous" or "Pseudonymous" Work: An author's contribution to a work is "anonymous" if that author is not identified on the copies or phonorecords of the work. An author's contribution to a work is "pseudonymous" if that author is identified on the copies or phonorecords under a fictitious name. If the work is "anonymous" you may: (1) leave the line blank; or (2) state "anonymous" on the line; or (3) reveal the author's identity. If the work is "pseudonymous" you may: (1) leave the line blank; or (2) give the pseudonym and identify it as such (for example: "Huntley Haverstock, pseudonym"); or (3) reveal the author's name, making clear which is the real name and which is the pseudonym (for example: "Henry Leek, whose pseudonym is Priam Farrel"). However, the citizenship or domicile of the author **must** be given in all cases.

Dates of Birth and Death: If the author is dead, the statute requires that the year of death be included in the application unless the work is anonymous or pseudonymous. The author's birth date is optional, but is useful as a form of identification. Leave this space blank if the author's contribution was a "work made for hire."

Author's Nationality or Domicile: Give the country of which the author is a citizen, or the country in which the author is domiciled. Nationality or domicile **must** be given in all cases.

Nature of Authorship: Give a brief general statement of the nature of this particular author's contribution to the work. Examples: "Painting"; "Photograph"; "Silk Screen Reproduction"; "Co-author of Cartographic Material"; "Technical Drawing"; "Text and Artwork."

3 SPACE 3: Creation and Publication

General Instructions: Do not confuse "creation" with "publication." Every application for copyright registration must state "the year in which creation of the work was completed." Give the date and nation of first publication only if the work has been published.

Creation: Under the statute, a work is "created" when it is fixed in a copy or phonorecord for the first time. Where a work has been prepared over a period of time, the part of the work existing in fixed form on a particular date constitutes the created work on that date. The date you give here should be the year in which the author completed the particular version for which registration is now being sought, even if other versions exist or if further changes or additions are planned.

Publication: The statute defines "publication" as "the distribution of copies or phonorecords of a work to the public by sale or other transfer of ownership, or by rental, lease, or lending"; a work is also "published" if there has been an "offering to distribute copies or phonorecords to a group of persons for purposes of further distribution, public performance, or public display." Give the full date (month, day, year) when, and the country where, publication first occurred. If first publication took place simultaneously in the United States and other countries, it is sufficient to state "U.S.A."

4 SPACE 4: Claimant(s)

Name(s) and Address(es) of Copyright Claimant(s): Give the name(s) and address(es) of the copyright claimant(s) in this work even if the claimant is the same as the author. Copyright in a work belongs initially to the author of the work (including, in the case of a work made for hire, the employer or other person for whom the work was prepared). The copyright claimant is either the author of the work or a person or organization to whom the copyright initially belonging to the author has been transferred.

Transfer: The statute provides that, if the copyright claimant is not the author, the application for registration must contain "a brief statement of how the claimant obtained ownership of the copyright." If any copyright claimant named in space 4 is not an author named in space 2, give a brief, general statement summarizing the means by which that claimant obtained ownership of the copyright. Examples: "By written contract"; "Transfer of all rights by author"; "Assignment"; "By will." Do not attach transfer documents or other attachments or riders.

5 SPACE 5: Previous Registration

General Instructions: The questions in space 5 are intended to find out whether an earlier registration has been made for this work and, if so, whether there is any basis for a new registration. As a rule, only one basic copyright registration can be made for the same version of a particular work.

Same Version: If this version is substantially the same as the work covered by a previous registration, a second registration is not generally possible unless: (1) the work has been registered in unpublished form and a second registration is now being sought to cover this first published edition; or (2) someone other than the author is identified as copyright claimant in the earlier registration, and the author is now seeking registration in his or her own name. If either of these two exceptions apply, check the appropriate box and give the earlier registration number and date. Otherwise, do not submit Form VA; instead, write the Copyright Office for information about supplementary registration or recordation of transfers of copyright ownership.

Changed Version: If the work has been changed, and you are now seeking registration to cover the additions or revisions, check the last box in space 5, give the earlier registration number and date, and complete both parts of space 6 in accordance with the instructions below.

Previous Registration Number and Date: If more than one previous registration has been made for the work, give the number and date of the latest registration.

6 SPACE 6: Derivative Work or Compilation

General Instructions: Complete space 6 if this work is a "changed version," "compilation," or "derivative work," and if it incorporates one or more earlier works that have already been published or registered for copyright, or that have fallen into the public domain. A "compilation" is defined as "a work formed by the collection and assembling of preexisting materials or of data that are selected, coordinated, or arranged in such a way that the resulting work as a whole constitutes an original work of authorship." A "derivative work" is "a work based on one or more preexisting works." Examples of derivative works include reproductions of works of art, sculptures based on drawings, lithographs based on paintings, maps based on previously published sources, or "any other form in which a work may be recast, transformed, or adapted." Derivative works also include works "consisting of editorial revisions, annotations, or other modifications" if these changes, as a whole, represent an original work of authorship.

Preexisting Material (space 6a): Complete this space **and** space 6b for derivative works. In this space identify the preexisting work that has been recast, transformed, or adapted. Examples of preexisting material might be "Grunewald Altarpiece"; or "19th century quilt design." Do not complete this space for compilations.

Material Added to This Work (space 6b): Give a brief, general statement of the **additional** new material covered by the copyright claim for which registration is sought. In the case of a derivative work, identify this new material. Examples: "Adaptation of design and additional artistic work"; "Reproduction of painting by photolithography"; "Additional cartographic material"; "Compilation of photographs." If the work is a compilation, give a brief, general statement describing both the material that has been compiled **and** the compilation itself. Example: "Compilation of 19th Century Political Cartoons."

7,8,9 SPACE 7, 8, 9: Fee, Correspondence, Certification, Return Address

Deposit Account: If you maintain a Deposit Account in the Copyright Office, identify it in space 7. Otherwise leave the space blank and send the fee of $10 with your application and deposit.

Correspondence (space 7): This space should contain the name, address, area code, and telephone number of the person to be consulted if correspondence about this application becomes necessary.

Certification (space 8): The application cannot be accepted unless it bears the date and the **handwritten signature** of the author or other copyright claimant, or of the owner of exclusive right(s), or of the duly authorized agent of the author, claimant, or owner of exclusive right(s).

Address for Return of Certificate (space 9): The address box must be completed legibly since the certificate will be returned in a window envelope.

MORE INFORMATION

Form of Deposit for Works of the Visual Arts

Exceptions to General Deposit Requirements: As explained on the reverse side of this page, the statutory deposit requirements (generally one copy for unpublished works and two copies for published works) will vary for particular kinds of works of the visual arts. The copyright law authorizes the Register of Copyrights to issue regulations specifying "the administrative classes into which works are to be placed for purposes of deposit and registration, and the nature of the copies or phonorecords to be deposited in the various classes specified." For particular classes, the regulations may require or permit "the deposit of identifying material instead of copies or phonorecords," or "the deposit of only one copy or phonorecord where two would normally be required."

What Should You Deposit? The detailed requirements with respect to the kind of deposit to accompany an application on Form VA are contained in the Copyright Office Regulations. The following does not cover all of the deposit requirements, but is intended to give you some general guidance.

For an Unpublished Work, the material deposited should represent the entire copyrightable content of the work for which registration is being sought.

For a Published Work, the material deposited should generally consist of two complete copies of the best edition. Exceptions: (1) For certain types of works, one complete copy may be deposited instead of two. These include greeting cards, postcards, stationery, labels, advertisements, scientific drawings, and globes; (2) For most three-dimensional sculptural works, and for certain two-dimensional works, the Copyright Office Regulations require deposit of identifying material (photographs or drawings in a specified form) rather than copies; and (3) Under certain circumstances, for works published in five copies or less or in limited, numbered editions, the deposit may consist of one copy or of identifying reproductions.

REQUEST FORM

Date:

Company: Phone:

Person spoken to:

Address:

Subject:

B/W: Color:

Use:

Deadline: Date order pulled:

Delivery Method: Date sent:

Method:

Research fee:

Price:

HOLDING FORM

TO:

For the convenience of both our offices, we would appreciate your assistance in the following: Please advise us in the "Remarks" section of any discrepancies in the number of photographs you have received and those listed on the attached Delivery Memo. List subject, photographer and serial number of all photographs you are holding. Check any other appropriate box, sign, date and return this form to us.

PHOTOGRAPHS BEING HELD

Total: b/w

                                                                                 color

Subject to permission being granted: Remarks:

Bill us for use

Bill us for service fee

Bill us for layout

Bill us for presentation

Bill us for artist reference

Holding for consideration

Photostated for possible use

None used; returning all herewith

Purchase order enclosed

Photostated for possible use

Company: Our Delivery #:

                                                             Delivery Date:

                                                             Date of Return:

Buyer:

Signature:

DELIVERY FOLLOW-UP FORM

Company Name:

Buyer:

Phone:

Regarding Deliver Memo [number], sent on [date]:

Date: Person spoken to:

Remarks:

INVOICE

TO: _____

Invoice #: _____

Delivery Memo #: _____

Date: _____

Terms: _____

Photographs   Rights Granted   Amount:

_____

_____

_____

_____

_____

_____

_____

_____

_____

_____

_____

_____

Total due: _____

_____

The terms and conditions set forth on the reverse side are deemed incorporated herein and made a part thereof.
Please note: a service charge of 2% per month will be charged to all balances over 30 days past due.

DELIVERY MEMO

TO: Date:
_____

                                                          Deliver #:
_____

_____

_____

_____

_____

Attention:
_____

Enclosed please find [number] b/w [format] and [number] color [format] photographs. This count shall be considered correct and the quality of the photographs considered satisfactory for reproduction if a copy of this memo is not immediately signed and returned. Terms and conditions of this delivery memo are set forth on the reverse side and are deemed and incorporated herein and made a part thereof.

Subject   b/w
_____

                                                          color
_____

Total:
_____

Acknowledged and accepted by:
_____

Please note: photos incorrectly credited are subject to an additional fee. All Photos are originals unless otherwise indicated.

Date
_____

Dear
_____

There has been no response to our second past-due notice for invoice [number], dated [   ].
_____

As stated in our Delivery Memo, reproduction of our photographs are not allowed until payment is received; thus, you are in violation of the copyright law. We would appreciate your prompt attention to this matter. Please send a check in the amount of [   ] to the above address.

Sincerely,

TERMS OF SUBMISSION AND USE

SUBMISSION

1. Photographs or transparencies (hereafter "photographs") may be held only for fourteen (14) days' approval. Unless a longer period is requested and granted by [your name] (hereafter "the photographer") in writing, a holding fee of $5.00 per week per color transparency and One ($1.00) per black and white print will be charged after such 14 day period and until their return.

2. Until submission of an invoice indicating recipient's right to use photographs according to terms hereinafter specified, the photographs may not be used in any way, including layouts, sketches, projectors or photostats.

3. Recipient accepts an insurer's liability herein for the safe and undamaged return of the photographs to photographer. Such photographs are to be returned by bonded messenger or by registered mail (return receipt requested), prepaid and fully insured.

   Recipient is accountable for loss or damage to the photographs delivered to it, from time of receipt until they are returned to photographer, and shall indemnify photographer against any loss or damage to photographs in transit or while in possession of Recipient. This agreement is not considered a bailment and is specifically conditioned upon the item so delivered being returned to Photographer in the same condition as delivered.

4. The monetary damage for loss or damage of an original color transparency or photograph shall be determined by the value of each individual photograph. Recipient agrees, however, that the reasonable value of such lost or damaged photograph or transparency shall be Fifteen Hundred ($1,500.) Dollars. Photographer agrees to the delivery of the goods herein only upon the express covenant and understanding by Recipient that the terms contained in this Paragraph 4 are material to this agreement. Recipient assumes full liability for its employees, agents, assigns, messengers and freelance researchers for the loss, damage or misuse of the photographs.

USE

5. Recipient accepts an insurer's liability herein for the safe and undamaged return of the photographs to Photographer. Recipient is solely accountable for loss or damage to photographs and will indemnify Photographer against any loss or damage, beginning with receipt by Recipient of such photographs until their return to, and receipt by Photographer. Such photographs are to be returned either by bonded messenger, or by registered mail (return receipt requested), prepaid and fully-insured.

6. Photographs used editorially shall display a credit line as indicated by Photographer. Recipient shall afford copyright protection to the photographer, which shall be immediately assigned to Photographer, upon request, without charge. Photographs and transparencies remain the property of the Photographer, unless specifically expressed in writing. Upon submission of an invoice, a license only is granted to use the photographs for the use cited on the invoice and for no other intention, unless such photographs are bought outright. Unless otherwise indicated, such use is granted for the United States only. Recipient does not acquire any right, title or interest to any photograph, including, without limitation, any electronic reproduction or promotional rights, and will not make, authorize or permit any use of the particular photograph(s) or plate(s) made therefrom other than as specified herein.

   Photographs are to be returned within 4 months after date of invoice, except in cases of outright purchase. Recipient agrees to pay, as reasonable price, the sum of $5 per week per photograph after such 4 month period to date of return.

7. The monetary damage for loss or damage of an original color transparency or photograph shall be decided by the value of each individual photograph. Recipient acknowledges, however, that the reasonable worth of such lost or damaged photograph or transparency shall be Fifteen Hundred ($1500) Dollars.

8. Photographer agrees to the delivery of the goods herein only upon the express agreement and understanding by Recipient that the Recipient accepts full liability for its employees, agents, assigns, messenger and freelance researchers for the loss, damage or misuse of the photographs.

9. No model releases or other releases exist on any photographs unless the existence of such release is specified in writing by Photographer. Recipient shall indemnify Photographer against all claims arising out of the use of any photographs where the existence of such release has not been specified in writing by Photographer. In any event, the limit of liability of Photographer shall be the sum paid to it per the invoice for the use of the particular photograph involved. Used will hold Photographer harmless from all claims for the use of the photographs, including defamatory use.

10. This agreement is not assignable or transferrable on the part of recipient.

11. Only the terms of use herein set forth shall be binding upon Photographer. No purported waiver of any of the terms herein shall be binding on Photographer unless subscribed in to in writing by Photographer.

12. Recipient agrees to promptly perform its commitment for payments and return of photographs hereunder. No rights are granted until payment is made to Photographer, even though Recipient has received an invoice.

13. Payment herein is to be net thirty (30) days. A service charge of two percent per month on any unpaid balance will be charged thereafter. Any claims for adjustment or rejection of terms must be made to Photographer within ten (10) days after receipt of invoice. In the event that any photographs are used by Recipient in publications, then Recipient shall send to Photographer on a semiannual basis (June 30th and December 31st), a certified statement setting forth the total number of sales, sublicenses, adaptations, translations and any other uses. Recipient shall provide Photographer with two (2) free copies of such publication immediately upon printing.

14. All rights not specifically granted herein to Recipient are reserved for Photographer's use and disposition without any limitations whatsoever.

15. Recipient agrees that the above terms are made pursuant to Article 2 of the Uniform Commercial code and agrees to be bound by same.

DISPUTES

16. Any and all disputes arising out of, under, or in connection with this agreement, including, without limitation, the validity, interpretation, performance and breach hereof, shall be settled by arbitration in [state] pursuant to the rule of the American Arbitration Association. Judgement upon the award rendered may be entered in the highest court of the Forum, State or Federal, having jurisdiction. This agreement, its validity and effect, shall be interpreted under and governed by the laws of the State of [   ].

17. If Photographer is caused to present claims or suit as a result of any breach of the above terms set forth, it shall be made whole for such reasonable legal fees and costs by recipient or user herein.

ADULT RELEASE

In consideration of my engagement as a model, upon the terms herewith stated, I hereby give to _____

_____

his heirs, legal representatives and assigns, those for whom_____

is acting, and those acting with his authority and permission:

a) the unrestricted right and permission to copyright and use, re-use, publish, and republish photographic portraits or pictures of me or in which I may be included intact or in part, composite or distorted in character or form, without restriction as to changes or transformations in conjunction with my own or a fictitious name, or reproduction hereof in color or otherwise, made through any and all media now or hereafter known for illustration, art, promotion, advertising, trade, or any other purpose whatsoever.

b) I also permit the use of any printed material in connection therewith.

c) I hereby relinquish any right that I may have to examine or approve the completed product or products or the advertising copy or printed matter that may be used in conjunction therewith or the use to which it may be applied.

d) I hereby release, discharge and agree to save harmless [photographer], his heirs, legal representatives or assigns, and all persons functioning under his permission or authority, or those for whom he is functioning, from any liability by virtue of any blurring, distortion, alteration, optical illusion, or use in composite form whether intentional or otherwise, that may occur or be produced in the taking of said picture or in any subsequent processing thereof, as well as any publication thereof, including without limitation any claims for libel or invasion of privacy.

e) I hereby affirm that I am over the age of majority and have the right to contract in my own name. I have read the above authorization, release and agreement, prior to its execution; I fully understand the contents thereof. This agreement shall be binding upon me and my heirs, legal representatives and assigns.

Dated: _____   Signed: _____

Address: _____

City: _____

State/Zip: _____

Phone: _____

Witness: _____

ADULT RELEASE
Simple Version

For valuable consideration, I hereby confer on _____ the absolute and irrevocable right and permission with respect to the photographs that he has taken of me or in which I may be included with others:

    a) To copyright the same in his own name or any other name that he may select;

    b) To use, re-use, publish and re-publish the same in whole or in part, separately or in conjunction with other photographs, in any medium now or hereafter known, and for any purpose whatsoever, including (but not by way of limitation) illustration, promotion, advertising and trade, and;

    c) To use my name in connection therewith if he so decides.

I hereby release and discharge [photographer] from all and any claims and demands ensuing from or in connection with the use of the photographs, including any and all claims for libel and invasion of privacy.

This authorization and release shall inure to the benefit of the legal representatives, licensees and assigns of _____ _____ , as well as the person(s) for whom he took the photographs.

I hereby affirm that I am of full age and have the right to contract in my own name. I have read the foregoing and fully understand the contents hereof. This release shall be binding upon me and my heirs, legal representatives and assigns.

Dated: _____

Signed: _____

Address: _____

City: _____

State/Zip: _____

Phone: _____

Witness: _____

MINOR RELEASE

For valuable consideration, I hereby confer _____

the unrestricted and irrevocable right and permission with respect to the photographs that he has taken of me or in which I may be included with others:

   a) To copyright the same in his own name or any other name that he may select;

   b) To use, re-use, publish and republish the same intact or in part, separately or in conjunction with other photographs, in any medium now or hereafter known, and for any purpose whatsoever, including (but not by way of limitation) illustration, promotion, advertising and trade, and;

   c) To use my name in connection therewith if he so decides.

I hereby release and discharge [photographer] from all and any claims and demands ensuing from or in connection with the use of the photographs, including any and all claims for libel and invasion of privacy.

This authorization and release shall inure to the benefit of the legal representatives, licensees and assigns of _____

_____

as well as the person(s) for whom he took the photographs.

I have read the foregoing and fully understand the contents hereof. I represent that I am the [parent/guardian] of the above named model. For value received, I hereby consent to the foregoing on his behalf.

Dated: _____   Parent or Guardian: _____

Minor's Name: _____   Address: _____

                                   City: _____

                                   State/Zip: _____

                                   Phone: _____

Witness: _____

PROPERTY RELEASE

For valuable consideration herein acknowledged as received, the undersigned being the legal owner of, or having the right to permit the taking and use of photographs of certain property designated as _____

_____

does grant to [photographer] his agents or assigns, the full rights to use such photographs and copyright same, in advertising, trade, or for any purpose.

    a) I also permit the use of any printed material in connection therewith.

    b) I hereby relinquish any right that I may have to examine or approve the completed product or products or the advertising copy or printed material that may be used in conjunction therewith or the use to which it may be applied.

    c) I hereby release, discharge and agree to save harmless [photographer] his heirs, legal representatives or assigns, and all persons functioning under his permission or authority, or those for whom he is functioning, from any liability by virtue of any blurring, distortion, alteration, optical illusion, or use in composite form whether intentional or otherwise, that may occur or be created in the taking of said picture or in any subsequent processing thereof, as well as any publication thereof, including without limitation any claims for libel or invasion of privacy.

    d) I hereby affirm that I am over the age of majority and have the right to contract in my own name. I have read the above authorization, release and agreement, prior to its execution; I fully understand the contents thereof. This agreement shall be binding upon me and my heirs, legal representatives and assigns.

Dated: _____

Signed: _____

Address: _____

City: _____

State/Zip: _____

Phone : _____

Witness: _____

PHOTOGRAPHER-AGENCY CONTRACT

I, (hereinafter referred to as "Photographer") attest that I am the sole and exclusive owner, now and in the future, of all original color transparencies, duplicates, negatives, prints, positives, and all other photographic matter (hereinafter referred to as "Images") delivered to you, (hereinafter referred to as "Agency"). Photographer attests that the Images do not knowingly infringe copyright, trademark, right of privacy or publicity and do not knowingly defame any third party. Photographer attests that he has the right to enter into an agreement with Agency and perform the obligations set forth herewith. Photographer and Agency agree that Agency shall lease and sell Images created by Photographer as delineated forthwith.

Both parties acknowledge that this Agreement is one of agency only and does not constitute an employment contract and that Agency is acting in the limited capacity of an independently retained agent on Photographer's behalf. Agency may not set itself out or bind Photographer contrary to the terms established hereof.

Photographer grants to Agency limited exclusivity as follows:

A. U.S. (regional, territories, possessions)

B. Foreign (list)

C. B/W ,Color

D. Stock,Assignment

E. All commitments of Agency under this agreement apply as well to the following sub-agents:
(list them)

Photographer agrees not to place the Images with another stock agency or picture selling medium as limited above. Exhibit A, attached hereto lists those clients who shall be deemed "House Accounts "and to whom Photographer may service exclusively with all fees to belong exclusively to Photographer. Agency grants that Photographer may sell or lease Images directly to these clients, or accept photographic assignments from them.

Agency shall have right to make all negotiations at its own discretion without prior consultation, except when outright purchase of originals is to be negotiated, which shall require Photographer's prior written approval, not to be reasonably withheld. Agency may not transfer to client any underlying rights in the Images.

Agency grants that it will not lease the use of any image for less than [amount] Dollars without the Photographer's written prior approval.

Agency agrees to carefully process all Images, by indexing them with reference to Photographer's name. The method of indexing must allow location of any Image within two (2) weeks. Agency will promptly refile all Images returned to it from clients.

All Images leased by Agency shall carry copyright notice in the name of the photographer. If a copyright notice is not affixed to the Images, Agency agrees to affix notice to Images before leasing Images to client. Agency agrees to demand in all agreements with clients, that in all uses, the Images shall be protected by copyright.

Agency accepts exclusive responsibility for all information Agency gives to clients concerning an Image that differs from information given to Agency by Photographer.

Agency will use its best efforts to protect and preserve the Images and exercise all due care in the handling of the Images.

In the event that Agency discovers unauthorized use, infringement, damage or loss to any of the Images, it will immediately inform photographer. Photographer retains right to control any action which proceeds therewith; and shall notify Agency in regard to the manner in which Photographer wants to proceed against such infringement. Photographer shall have the right to cause Agency to be joined as a part in any litigation concerning the Images. Payment of all costs (including lawyer's fees) and proceeds from any such case shall be divided equally between Photographer and Agency.

Agency acknowledges that it will provide safe conditions for long term storage, care and retrieval of Images; this shall include shelter from damp, heat, dust and overexposure to light.

Photographer agrees to accurately caption and affix copyright notice in Photographer's name to all Images. Photographer will notify Agency which Images have Model Releases; a copy of which shall be given to Agency upon request. Agency accepts all responsibility for the use of Images that do not contain a notation regarding the existence of a model release; Agency indemnifies Photographer from any and all damages incurred by Agency, Photographer or third parties in connection with such uses.

Photographer agrees to deliver to Agency such Images as Photographer deems will advance the purposes of this contract. Agency shall review same and within thirty (30) days thereafter return to Photographer all Images, designating those Images which Agency deems appropriate for license pursuant to its Agency obligations hereunder. Images so designated shall be re-delivered to Agency and the use of same shall be governed by this agreement. Both Photographer and Agency agree that time is of the essence in fulfilling the obligations stated herewith promptly after the execution of this Agreement.

Images not selected and not representing so-called "dupes " or "similars " to Images designated by Agency may be sold, licensed or used by Photographer in Photographer's sole discretion.

"Dupes " shall be defined as duplicates, facsimiles or other reproduction of Images, whether created by Photographer, Agency, permissible sub-agent or clients; all "Dupes " remain exclusive property of Photographer, subject only to permissible licenses, regardless of which party has created such "Dupes". Photographer grants/denies [choose one] permission to license the use of "Dupes " to clients. Agency agrees that it will not allow clients to create "Dupes " without Photographer's prior written approval. Agency acknowledges that it will account to Photographer for "Dupes " in all respects as if they were Images licensed under this Agreement and all provisions of this Agreement apply to such "Dupes."

Agency may use the services of foreign sub-agents in connection with the license of the Images only with the prior written approval of Photographer. Agency agrees to first provide Photographer with name and address of proposed sub-agent. The percentage of gross billings shall not exceed that percentage of gross billings specifically stated as Agency's compensation below; this includes Agency commission or fees, fees of Agency and all permissible sub-agents.

Agency will be permitted to retain [amount] percent (%) of the gross billings in connection with the license of the Images in consideration of the services furnished by Agency hereunder and the performance of its obligations hereunder. "Gross billings " shall be defined as all revenue, of whatever nature and from whatever source, derived from license of the Images, and shall include, without limitation, holding fees and interest assessed, but shall not be deemed to include so-called "service fees. " The only permissible deductions from gross billings are bad debts and other uncollectible sums actually incurred and reasonable currency conversion costs. Agency agrees to hold in trust for the Photographer all sums received as gross billings from the license of the Images; these sums are subject only to the retention by Agency of its commission as set forth above.

Agency agrees to provide payment and a detailed statement of the licensing by Agency of the Images on the following basis:

(every 30, 60 or 90 days)

This statement will include the gross billings, the deductions from gross billings, date payment received, name of client, rights granted, and identity of image.

Upon reasonable notice and during regular business hours, Photographer or his designated representative shall have the right to inspect Agency's books and records and to make extracts thereof as same relate to Photographer's Images. If the result of such an audit

is the discovery that Agency has underpaid Photographer by an amount equal to or in excess of five percent (5%) of all monies due to Photographer, then Agency shall bar all costs and expenses of such audit as well as remit to Photographer all past due sums with interest to date. The foregoing shall not be deemed to be a waiver of or limitation upon Photographer's other rights or remedies in the event of such underpayment.

Agency acknowledges that it shall be solely responsible for the collection and payment of any and all taxes whether in the nature of a sales, personal property, excise, remittance, or other tax which is or may become due and payable in connection with any license of the Images pursuant to the terms of this Agreement.

Agency shall use all reasonable efforts (including inquiries with appropriate trade associations) to locate Photographer in the event statements are returned unclaimed. Photographer agrees to provide Agency with an alternate address for notice purposes on the signature page of this Agreement, in order to assist Agency in this endeavor. In the event that Photographer cannot be located, notwithstanding Agency's efforts to locate him, Agency shall deposit any portion of gross billings due to Photographer in a separate interest bearing account (into which account Agency may deposit sums due to the Photographers whom Agency is unable to locate.) Such sums shall remain on deposit for a period of five (5) years or such longer period of time as may be permissible by law. If Agency is not contacted by Photographer or his personal representative before the expiration of such time period, the sums on deposit with Agency shall be treated according to the laws of the State of in regard to abandoned property.

In the event Photographer shall die during the Term hereof or shall become disabled or incompetent, Photographer or, in the case of death or incompetency, Photographer's personal representative, shall have the right, exercisable by sixty (60) days prior written notice to Agency, to cause this agreement and Agency's authorization hereunder to terminate. Except as may otherwise be provided herein, this Agreement shall be binding upon and shall inure to the benefit of the respective heirs, executors, administrators, successors and assigns of the parties hereto.

Agency and Photographer agree to indemnify and hold the other party harmless from and against all final judgments and settlements with consent (hereafter collectively referred to as "claims") which may arise as a result of a breach or alleged breach of the party granting the indemnity (hereinafter the "Indemnitor") of any representation, warranty or undertaking to be performed by such Indemnitor. The party be indemnified (hereinafter the Indemnitee") shall promptly notify the Indemnitor of any such claim, and the Indemnitor shall thereupon have the right to undertake the defense of such claim.

The Indemnitee shall have the right, but not the obligation, to be represented by counsel of its choice and participate in such defense at is sole cost and expense. The Indemnitee shall not settle any such claim without the prior written approval of the Indemnitor. Anything to the contrary contained herein notwithstanding, in the event Photographer is called upon to indemnify Agency pursuant to the foregoing indemnity, Photographer shall not be liable for any monetary sums in excess of the share of gross billings theretofore received by Photographer from Agency pursuant to this Agreement.

Agency acknowledges that it may not assign this Agreement without the prior written consent of Photographer. Any assignment in contravention of the foregoing prohibition shall be deemed null and void. Photographer shall have the right to assign this Agreement to any corporation in which Photographer is a principal stockholder, and to assign Photographer's share of gross bills earned hereunder.

This Agreement and all matters collateral thereto shall be construed according to the laws of State of [name], and any controversy arising hereunder shall be litigate solely in a court of competent jurisdiction of such state.

This Agreement incorporates the entire understanding of the parties concerning the subject matter contained herein and may not be modified, amended or otherwise changed in any respect except by a separate writing signed by the party to be charged therewith.

Agency shall be deemed to be in default of its obligations if any of its representations or warranties contained herein or any other undertaking on its part to be performed hereunder are breached; and if Agency fails to cure such breach within ten (10) days after receipt of notice from Photographer specifying same; if a petition in a bankruptcy or for reorganization is filed by or against Agency; or if Agency makes an assignment for the benefit of its creditors; or if Agency fails to pay its general creditors promptly; or if a receiver, liquidator, trustee or custodian is appointed for all or a substantial part of Agency's property, and the order of appointment is not vacated within thirty (30) days; or if Agency assigned or encumbers this Agreement contrary to the terms hereof; or if agency ceases to conduct its business or sells or merges substantially all of its assets.

Photographer shall be allowed to immediately terminate Agency's authorization under this Agreement in the event of any act of default as set forth above, in addition to any other remedy Photographer may have; Photographer shall thereupon be relieved of any continuing obligation it may have to Agency. All business activity with respect to the Images shall immediately cease and Agency will promptly retrieve and deliver to Photographer all Images as required below.

Agency shall use all reasonable efforts to promptly retrieve and turn over to Photographer all of the Images then in Agency's possession no matter where such Images may be located, upon the expiration or termination of this Agreement. Agency agrees that such retrieval and delivery to Photographer requires no more than a period of three (3) months after termination, with respect to Images located in Agency's files, and one (1) year after expiration or termination with respect to Images in the possession of Clients at the time of such expiration or termination.

During the retrieval period after termination or expiration, Agency shall diligently return to Photographer all Images returned by Clients. If Images are still outstanding one (1) year after termination or expiration, Agency shall provide Photographer with written notification specifically setting forth the identification of Image, and address and name of client who is holding Image.

Upon reasonable prior notice, for purposes of furtherance of Photographer's professional interest (i.e., exhibitions), or in the event Agency does not comply with its retrieval and return obligations pursuant to this paragraph, Photographer shall have direct access to Agency's files.

This agreement shall begin as of the date set forth below and shall continue for a period of three (3) years (the "Initial Period"). Agency shall have the right, at least thirty (30) days prior to the expiration of the Initial Period, to notify Photographer of its desire to renew the agreement for an additional period of one (1) year period. Notwithstanding the foregoing, Photographer may , upon receipt of any such thirty (30) day notice, notify Agency of its desire to terminate this Agreement. The Agreement shall thereafter terminate at the expiration of the then current Term. The Initial Period and each renewal period are collectively referred to herein as the "Term".

Photographer shall have the right to terminate this Agreement on thirty (30) days prior written notice to Agency if Agency fails to derive gross billings from Photographer's Images for a period of one (1) year.

In witness whereof the parties have executed this Agreement _____ on 19____

Agency _____   Photographer_____

Address_____   Address _____

_____   _____

BOOK PUBLISHING CONTRACT

Agreement made on [full date] between [name of publisher]   (hereinafter referred to as "the publisher"and [name of photographer]   (hereinafter referred to as "the photographer").

The Photographer hereby grants to the Publisher, and the Publisher hereby agrees to, a limited license to reproduce, publish and vend a hardcover edition of a book presently entitled [name of book] (hereinafter referred to as "said Book"), containing certain photographs by the Photographer (hereinafter referred to as "said photographs") upon the following terms and conditions:

1. The Publisher's rights hereunder shall be for a period beginning [date] and ending [date], unless discontinued sooner as provided herein.

2. The license granted to the Publisher hereunder is exclusively for the Publisher's hardcover edition of said Book. The license granted hereunder is for one - time, nonexclusive, reproduction use of said photographs in English-language printing in the following countries [list of countries].

The photographer shall present to the publisher [number] photographs (whether black and white or color, or any combination) on or before [date]. The Publisher will choose the photographs to be used in said book in [number] months from the receipt of said photographs, with those photographs not chosen to be returned promptly to the photographer. Upon return of the photographs, the photographer will be notified which photographs have been chosen, and an inventory of such photographs shall then be placed in this agreement by reference thereto. The photographer shall have freedom to use all unchosen photographs in any manner whatsoever without limitation; all unchosen photographs shall be excluded from the scope of this agreement.

All photographs so chosen by the Publisher for use in said Book will be returned to the Photographer no later than thirty (30) days after the plates are made. Such plates are to be made by [date]   . Said book is to be published no later than [date], with a minimum of [number] copies so published and distributed.

The Publisher shall not acquire any right, title, or interest in or to said photographs and shall not create, entitle, or permit any use of said photographs other than as specified herein. Without circumscribing the generality of the foregoing, said photographs may not be used in any way, including, without limitation, projections, layouts, sketches, and photostats, except on the terms designated herein.

3. The Publisher shall publish and distribute said Book at its own expense, in the style and manner and at the price which it deems best befits its sale.

Before publication, however, said Book shall be submitted in its entirety to the Photographer, including, without limitation, the text, its title, its photographs, and the contents of its covers, and said Book shall only be published in the form approved by the Photographer. Any approval by the Photographer, shall not in any way limit, negate, or affect the provisions contained in this agreement.

4. The Publisher shall pay to the Photographer, or his duly authorized representative specified in writing by the Photographer, upon the execution of this agreement, the following nonreturnable advance, which shall be charged against the Photographer's royalties set forth the following paragraph hereof [amount of advance.]

5. The Publisher shall pay to the Photographer the following percentages of the Publisher's U.S. suggested retail list price:

Ten (10%) on first 5,000 copies sold.

Twelve and One Half (12 1/2%) on next 5,000 copies sold.

Fifteen (15%) percent on all copies sold in excess of the aforesaid 10,000 copies.

It is understood that the suggested retail list price shall be deemed to be not less than $ [amount] for the purpose of computing the royalties to be paid hereunder.

6. The Photographer shall be paid accrued royalties semiannually, within thirty (30) days after June thirtieth and December thirty-first of each calendar year, with payment to be accompanied by detailed statements of all sales, licenses, accrued royalties, and deductions.

Books of accounts containing accurate records of all transactions involving the subject matter of this agreement and of all sums of money received and disbursed in connection therewith, shall be kept by the Publisher in its place of primary business. The Photographer or his duly authorized representative shall have the right at any time and without limitation to examine and audit the Publisher's books, records, and accounts in order to authenticate or clarify any and all such statements, accounting, and payments. The photographer shall carry the cost of such inspection, unless errors of accounting total five (5%) percent or more of the total sums paid or payable to the Photographer shall be found to his detriment, in which case the Publisher shall carry the expense of such inspection.

Publisher shall pay the Photographer any advances or royalties received by Publisher from book clubs or other licensees (if applicable) within thirty days after Publisher receives such payments, included with a copy of the statement of account provided by such licensee to Publisher.

Regardless of anything in this paragraph to the contrary, any sum of One Thousand ($1,000) Dollars or more which may become due to the Photographer (after the Publisher shall have recouped its advance hereunder) shall be paid by the Publisher to the Photographer within thirty (30) days after the Publisher shall have received such sum.

7. The Publisher shall be responsible for the safe return of all photographs to the Photographer and shall indemnify the Photographer against any loss or damage to such photographs (including those not selected for use in said Book) in transit or while in possession of the Publisher, its agents, employees, messengers, printer, or assigns.

The monetary figure for loss or damage of an original transparency or photograph shall be determined by the value of each individual photograph. The publisher and Photographer concur that the fair and reasonable value of such lost or damaged transparency shall be One Thousand Five Hundred ($1,500.00) Dollars for a color transparency or black and white negative. The Publisher shall be liable for all acts of its employees, agents, assigns, messengers, printer, and freelance researchers for all loss, damage, or misuse of said photographs by the Photographer hereunder. Any such payment shall not, however, entitle the Publisher to any right, title, or interest in or to said Materials so lost or damaged.

8. No books or other material related to said Book shall be distributed without the Photographer's credit as approved by him. The Photographer shall be credited on the dust jacket, cover, title page, and interior of said Book, as well as in advertising under the control of the Publisher, all in size, type, and prominence not less than that afforded any other person or part appearing thereon, and all subject to the Photographer's final and absolute approval.

9. Said Book shall be published with due notice of copyright in the name of the Photographer and shall be duly registered in the Copyright Office of the United States of America. Without limiting the foregoing, all copyrights under the Berne Convention, the Universal Copyright Office of the United States of America, and the Buenos Aires Treaty will be secured. In no event shall said Book be published without a copyright of the photographs in the name of the Photographer. The Publisher will take all steps necessary, without cost to the photographer, to secure such copyrights, including any renewal copyrights, if applicable, as well as to prosecute or defend any infringement actions as stated within with agreement.

10. The Publisher shall provide the Photographer with twenty (20) copies of said Book as published, free of any cost or charge to the Photographer whatsoever, for the photographer's own use. If the Photographer needs additional copies to those above, the Publisher shall provide such additional copies to the Photographer at a reduction of forty (40%) percent from the retail selling price or at the Publisher's actual publishing cost for same, whichever is less.

11. All notices which either party may request or be required to relay to the other shall be sent by prepaid registered mail and addressed to the parties as follows:
Publisher:

Photographer:

12. Only when copies are obtainable and offered for sale in the U.S. through normal retail channels and listed in the catalog issued to the trade by the Publisher shall Said Book be deemed "in print". Reproduction of copies by reprographic processes or availability by any medium or means other than the hardcover edition referred to above shall not be deemed "in print".

If Publisher neglects to keep Said Book in print, the Photographer may at any time thereafter request in writing that the Publisher place the Book in print. The Publisher must notify the Photographer within sixty (60) days from receipt of such request, whether it plans to comply with said request. This agreement shall automatically end and all rights granted to the Publisher shall thereupon automatically revert to the Photographer if Publisher fails to give such notice, or having done so, fails to place the Book in print within six (6) months after receipt of said request by Photographer.

If, after the first printing and distribution of said Book, the Publisher determines to cancel any further publication of said Book, it shall give immediate notice of such determination to the Photographer, and the Photographer shall have the right to purchase from the Publisher the plates for said Book at one-fourth (1/4) of the original amount, including the initial compositions, and the Publishers's stock at one-quarter (1/4) of the list price thereof. If the Photographer shall not take over the said plates, engravings, illustrations, and/or copies of said Book and pay for same within ninety (90) days, then the Publisher shall destroy the items not taken and shall supply the Photographer with an affidavit of destruction thereof. In any event, the Publisher's contract for payments hereunder to the Photographer shall nevertheless persevere.

13. The Publisher agrees and understands that the Photographer makes no warranty, express or implied, and the Publisher hereby agrees to indemnify, defend, save, and hold harmless the Photographer, his successors, and assigns, against any and all claims, losses, costs, damages, or expenses, including

reasonable counsel fees and expenses, which shall accrue or be claimed against the Photographer or his successors and assigns, or any others, by reason of the use of said photographs hereunder or other conduct by the Publisher in connection with any rights granted by the Photographer hereby, as indicated by the Publisher's acceptance of the photographs hereunder.

14. Photographer and Publisher shall have the right to act jointly in an action for an infringement by a third party of any rights granted to the Publisher hereunder. The costs of the action will be shared equally if both Publisher and Photographer participate and they shall recoup such costs from any sums recovered in the action, with the balance of the proceeds to be equally divided between them. Each party will inform the other of infringements coming to its attention. If the Photographer decides not to participate in such action, the Publisher will continue and will carry all costs and expenses which shall be recouped from any damages recouped from the infringement, and the balance of such damages shall be distributed equally between the parties.

15. Any dispute or claim originating out of or regarding this agreement or the violation thereof shall be settled by arbitration in [name of state], in accordance with the rules of the American Arbitration Association, and judgement upon the award rendered by the Arbitrator(s) may be registered in any court having jurisdiction thereof.

16. The Photographer may independently assign his right to acquire income under this agreement. The Publisher may not assign this agreement, either voluntarily or by operation of law, without the prior written consent of the Photographer. Any such assignment, if approved of by the Photographer, shall not relieve the Publisher of its responsibilities hereunder.

17. In acknowledgment of the importance of punctuality in the performance by the Publisher of its obligations hereunder, the Publisher agrees that if it neglects to pay promptly the royalties hereunder, or if the Publisher neglects to conform or comply with any other terms or conditions hereunder, the Photographer shall have the right, either personally or by his duly authorized representative, to advise the Publisher of such default. If fourteen (14) days pass after the sending of such notice without the default's having been rectified, this agreement shall thereupon discontinue without affecting the Photographer's rights to compensation or damages regarding any claims or causes of action the Photographer may have.

18. All rights not specifically granted herein to the Publisher are retained for the Photographer's use and disposition without any limitation whatsoever, regardless of the extent to which same are competitive with the Publisher or the license granted hereunder. This includes, without limitation, all individual uses of the photographs hereunder.

19. Nothing enclosed in this agreement shall be deemed to constitute the Publisher and the Photographer as partners, joint venturers, of fiduciaries, or give the Publisher a property interest, whether of a legal or an equitable nature, in any of the Photographer's assets.

20. A waiver by either party of any of the terms and conditions of this agreement shall not be deemed or construed to be a waiver of such terms or conditions for the future, or of any subsequent breach thereof. All remedies, rights, undertakings, obligations, and agreements enclosed in this agreement shall be cumulative, and none of them shall be in limitation of any other remedy, right, undertaking, obligation, or agreement of either party.

21. In case of the Publisher's bankruptcy, receivership, or assignment for benefit of creditors, the rights of publication shall revert to the Photographer.

22. This agreement and all its terms and conditions, and all rights herein, shall insure to the benefit of, and shall be binding upon, the parties hereto and their respective legal representatives, successors and assigns.

23. All rights not specifically granted herein to the Publisher are retained for the Photographer's use and disposition without any limitation whatsoever, regardless of the extent to which same are competitive with the Publisher or the license granted hereunder. This includes, without limitation, all individual uses of the photographs hereunder.

24. This agreement and all matters or issues collateral thereof shall be interpreted under, and governed by, the laws of the state of [name of state].

This agreement constitutes the complete agreement between the parties hereto and cannot be altered or discontinued verbally. No alterations, amendments or assignment thereof shall be binding except in writing signed by both parties.

This agreement is not binding on the Photographer unless and until a copy thereof actually signed by both the Photographer and the Publisher is delivered to the Photographer and payment of the advance is made.

In witness whereof, the parties hereto have executed this agreement as of the day and year first written above.

By: (publisher)_____   By [photographer]: _____

Title: _____   Title: _____

Chapter 13

FOR MORE INFORMATION

THE ART + BUSINESS OF CREATIVE SELF-PROMOTION. by Herring & Fulton. How communications professionals can gain a competitive edge and increase profits. Scores of self-promotion pieces-posters, ads, direct mail, portfolios-with commentary and text. 144 pp. 8 1/4 x 11
Hardbound $27.50

PROFESSIONAL BUSINESS PRACTICES IN PHOTOGRAPHY. Since it first appeared in 1973, *Professional Business Practices In Photography* has become the most vital tool at the command of the photographic professional. The completely revised edition is even more distinguished in its timeliness and completeness. It is state-of-art; the only one of its kind.

The 1986 edition, in addition to a thorough revision of existing materials to ensure up-to-date accuracy, has new sections on: The New Technologies, Architectural Photography, Updated regional surveys. ". . . the standard reference" said *Publisher's Weekly*; "The top authority on photographers' rights." ". . . the last word in the business" said *The San Diego Union*, and from *Creative Communicator*: ". . . the 'Bible' of photography! A must!"

Today, more than ever before, *Professional Business Practices In Photography* is essential if the professional is to avoid the treacherous pitfalls of a demanding business. Researched and written by the country's leading photographers, the fully revised edition of the Business Practices Book is an ongoing contribution by the American Society of Magazine Photographers to professionalism and expertise in the business and art of photography. 9 x 12. 112 pp.
Softcover $27.00

ASMP STOCK PHOTOGRAPHY HANDBOOK. The Authoritative & Definitive Directory for established professionals, buyers of photography, talented amateur photographers. Some three years in the making, the ASMP Stock Photography Handbook stands alone as the most comprehensive of reference manuals yet published on the subject. Each chapter is complete, authoritative, and represents a compilation of data supplied by more than 300 top professionals in this country and abroad.
Softcover $24.00

THE CREATIVE BLACK BOOK 1989. An industry phenomenon, the bible of the advertising photographer and illustrator. A resource directory with advertising, now in it's 18th year. 153 pp., 1200 in color 6 1/2x10 3/4
Hardbound $100.00

CREATIVE BLACK BOOK, Portfolio edition 1300 pp. 1200 color 6 1/2x10 3/4
Hardbound $70.00

CREATIVE STRATEGY. by Butsch and Cafiero. A marketing manifesto by the directors of creative access, mailing list managers for creative marketing. Basic advice for mailing promotions for the freelance photographer from experts in direct mail marketing. 56 pp. 5 1/2x8 1/4
Softcover $12.95

GETTING IT PRINTED. by Beach, Shepro, and Russon. A fresh, clear, jargon-free approach to working with printers and graphic arts services to insure quality, stay on schedule, and control costs. Features included forms for organizing jobs and writing specs, glossary, and anecdotes from printers and people who buy printing. 236 pp. 8 1/2x11
Softcover $29.50

GETTING TO THE TOP IN PHOTOGRAPHY. by Gambaccini. Practical advice and interviews with leading pros in advertising, people, sports, portraiture, fashion and entertainment photography. Career advice for the beginning and established pro. 144 pp.
Softcover $14.95

HOW TO SHOOT & SELL ANIMAL PHOTOS. by Walter Chandoha. Photographers will learn: how to take photos that go beyond just technically good to have life and charm, how to get animals to cooperate during photo sessions to capture the poses and expressions clients want or need, what indoor and outdoor equipment and lighting to use. S $16.00

HOW YOU CAN MAKE $50,000 A YEAR AS A NATURE PHOTOJOURNALIST. by Bill Thomas. A veteran nature photographer shares all the ways to make money and marketing techniques 192 pp. 150 photos 8x10
Softcover $18.00

HOW TO CREATE AND SELL PHOTO PRODUCTS. by Mike and Carol Werner. Creating and selling products featuring one's photos-such as clocks, placemats, or bookmarks-can be a profitable business, and this thorough guide is packed with diagrams and illustrations for over 30 products, plus advice for setting up a photo business.
Softcover $15.00

MODEL RELEASE FORMS. 100 Ready to use forms to protect the photographer and model from lawsuits. Easy to use, complete, and necessary for most advertising photography and many stock photo agency submissions. 8 1/2x11 $3.95

THE PERFECT PORTFOLIO. by Henrietta Brackman. A finely tailored portfolio is the most important sales tool for anyone who wants to sell his or her photographs. These understandable, step-by- step instructions teach the secrets that the professionals use in preparing their own portfolios. You'll be able to create your own, personal portfolio that will start your career off right-and keep it going.
Softcover $18.95

PHOTO MARKETING HANDBOOK by Cason and Lawrence. What does it take to successfully sell your stock photos worldwide? The most up-to-date market listings of stock photo agencies in the US, Europe, Asia and Australia. Includes postcard, poster, book publishers. Concise text covers everything the serious amateur and professional photographer needs to sell stock photographs: organizing, finding the right markets, legal rights, etc. Contains business forms (releases, contracts, submission memos). How to publish a photo book. Tips from working pro's, agents, and editors. 160pp 8 1/2 x 11
Softcover $18.95

PHOTOGRAPHERS ALMANAC. by Miller and Nelson. An indispensible guide to commercial photography: dealing with galleries, contracts, running a business, purchasing equipment, processing, expert advice for the pro or would be professional photographer. 277 pp. 8 1/2x11
Hardbound $12.95

THE PHOTOGRAPHER'S COMPLETE GUIDE TO EXHIBITION SALES SPACES. by Photographers Arts Center. Over 1,300 places to Sell and Exhibit Your Photographs for the fine art photographer. Complete guide to dealers, galleries, museums, corporate collections, and publishers in the USA & abroad. 130 pp. 9x12 S $20.00

THE PHOTOGRAPHER'S COMPUTER HANDBOOK. by B. Nadine Orabona. Orabona, a freelance photographer and data processing consultant, shares specific procedures for completely computerizing a freelance or stock photography business-how to select hardware and software and use a computer to handle everything from stock filing and retrieval to photo captioning, equipment inventory, scheduling, pricing, and business correspondence.
Softcover $16.00

THE PHOTOGRAPHER'S GUIDE TO GETTING & HAVING A SUCCESSFUL EXHIBITION. by Robert Persky. This book presents a clear and concise plan of action that starts with how to make contacts with exhibition spaces and continues with information on written agreements, budgeting, announcements, invitations and publicity. 8 1/2x11.
Softcover $24.95

THE PHOTOGRAPHER'S GUIDE TO MARKETING AND SELF-PROMOTION. by Maria Piscopo. Everything photographers need to know to plan and execute their own personalized self-promotion campaign-and sell more of their photos! Covers in detail everything a photographer needs to market and promote a photography career...personal promotion campaigns...press releases...presentations...negotiating, hiring a rep, etc. Interviews with photographers and samples included. 128 pp.
Softcover $16.95

PHOTOGRAPHY BEST SELLERS. by Ong. One Hundred of the top money making stock photos from a leading stock agency...each photo is presented with complete reports of sales volumes, background, *times sold, etc. The 100 images pictured have been purchased over 5,000 times and have produced over two million dollars in sales. A real eye-opener, this book is a fascinating look into the stock photo business. 9x11 120 photos.
Hardbound $29.95

PHOTOGRAPHY FOR THE ART MARKET. by K. Marx. A working guide the "art" photographer: prints, posters, fine art books, paper products, etc. Interviews with buyers and sellers, range of prices. 144 pp. 8 1/4x11 color ills.
Softcover $18.95

PICTURES THAT SELL - A Guide to Successful Stock Photography. by Daffurn and Hicks. A sophisticated look into the world of the professional stock photographer-for those photographers who want to gain a profitable insight into the picture-selling business, this practical and profusely illustrated guide will prove invaluable. 189 pp. 9x12. 244 color
Hardbound $24.00

THE PROFESSIONAL PHOTOGRAPHER'S BUSINESS GUIDE. by Frederick W. Rosen. this in-depth practical handbook shows how to start a photographic business, how to run it successfully and how to expand. Interviews with top photographers offer advice to the photographer just out and to the professional ready to grow. 192 pp. 6x9. 25 B&W illus.
Softcover $13.00

PROFESSIONAL PHOTOGRAPHERS SURVIVAL GUIDE. by Rotkin. "This is the first book that addresses the problems of the freelance photographer...A must for anyone in the business of producing, selling, or using photography."...Arnold Drapkin, TIME magazine. 320 pages 6x9
Softcover $12.95

PROMOTING YOURSELF AS A PHOTOGRAPHER. by Rosen. The first book to give professional photographers step-by-step programs to promote themselves and their work. Both free and paid promotion techniques are covered. 208 pp. 7x9 1/2 55 photos
Softcover $16.95

PUBLISH YOUR PHOTO BOOK. by Bill Owens. (A guide to self- publishing). The reality of the photographic book publishing world, by the author of four photographic books. A step by step primer on commercial publishing, finding a printer, books and money, letters from self-publishers, publicity, distribution, and legal matters. 8x9. 140 pp. B&W illus.
Softcover $9.00

SECRETS OF STUDIO STILL LIFE PHOTOGRAPHY. by Gary Perweiller. "...a wonderful learning tool, one that should be of interest to the aspiring commercial photographer, the assistant and the generalist...to the professional photographer doing still-life work too." *Photo District News.* 144 pp. 8 1/4x11. 120 color plates. 50 line drawings. Gloss.
Softcover $18.95

NEW EDITION! SELL & RESELL YOUR PHOTOS. by Engh. This consistent bestseller is now completely revised and updated to continue helping photographers sell their photos-again and again-to-markets nationwide by phone and mail. Experienced advice getting best prices, recordkeeping, rights, copyrights, taxes, self-promotion. 336 pp. 6x9.
Hardbound $16.95

NEW! SELLING PHOTOGRAPHS. by Lou Jacobs, Jr. Determining your rates and understanding your rights. Explaining clearly and thoroughly all of the legalities of the photographic business world. Explains precisely how much a photographer should charge. 192 pp. 7x9 1/2
Softcover $16.95

SELLING YOUR PHOTOGRAPHY. No matter how far you've come as a photographer, *Selling Your Photography* serves as a one-of-a- kind volume. It covers in depth the three crucial areas of the photographer-Marketing, Business and Law, and covers them completely. 256 pp. 6x9"
Hardbound $16.00

SHOOTING FOR STOCK. by Schaub. How to create, organize, and market photographs that will sell again and again. An up-to-date analysis of this booming market..from what sells to how to sell it. 144 pp. 8 1/4x11 65 photos.
Softcover $19.00

STARTING AND SUCCEEDING IN-YOUR OWN PHOTOGRAPHY BUSINESS. by Jeanne Thwaites. This no-nonsense guide to starting a photography studio truly leaves nothing to chance. Thwaites gives complete details on what steps to take, including: the rent vs. buy decision, choosing a location; rounding up equipment; finances; handling employees; advertising; pricing; insurance; and collecting debts. She covers every angle and obstacle to help readers start and keep their business running smoothly and profitably.
Hardbound $18.95

STOCK PHOTOGRAPHY. by Ellis Herwig. This is the only book on selling photographs that tells photographers how to see marketable pictures as well as how to sell them-not just one time but over and over again. Sound, well-thought-out professional advice rounds out the book. The author surveys the technical aspects of shooting stock photography.
Softcover $12.95

STOCK WORKBOOK 2. The 2nd edition of the largest directory of stock images ever published. Filled with thought provoking, idea-generating images in full color, it features carefully selected samples from major stock agencies; superbly reproduced in large format. Organized by agency, cross-indexed to hundreds of subjects. 420 + pp. Over 2500 color photographs. 9x12
Softcover $35.00

Billing Address: _____   **Shipping Address:** _____

_____   _____

_____   _____

_____   _____

_____   _____

Quantity	Book Name	Unit Cost	Total Cost

There is a 15% discount on 3 or more books ordered at one time.   **Subtotal:** _____

Tax %: _____

S/H/I: _____

Total: _____

Shipping is $2.00 for the first book and $.50 for each additional book.

Check, Money Orders, Mastercard, and Visa accepted. Foreign orders by credit card or check drawn on an American bank in US dollars.

Mail order to:
Gould Trading
22 E 17th Street
New York, New York 10003   USA

Or call:
(212) 243-2306 for more information
(800) 367-4854 for orders in the US only

Chapter 14
ORGANIZATIONS THAT OFFER HELP

PHOTOGRAPHERS' ORGANIZATIONS

Always, your best source for finding the professional who can help you is a friend whose needs have been the same as yours. Chapter 11 offers suggestions for ways of finding a lawyer; in addition to those sources, consider asking the photography or art department of your local college or university for the names of people or groups who might be of help.

The following are some of the best-known and largest of the photographers' organizations.

Advertising Photographers of America (A.P.A.)
118 East 25th Street
New York, NY 10010

**American Society of
Magazine Photographers (A.S.M.P.)**
419 Park Avenue South
New York, NY 10016

Association of Professional Color Laboratories
603 Lansing Avenue
Jackson, MI 49202

Biological Photographic Assn.
6650 Northwest Highway
Chicago, IL 60631

Boston Press Photographers Association
Box 122
Boston, MA 02101

California Press Photographers Association
2452 40th Avenue
Sacramento, CA 95822

Canadian Photographic Trade Association
94 Lakeshore Road East
Mississauga, Ontario L5G 1E3 Canada

Chicago Press Photographers Association
211 East Chicago Avenue
Chicago, IL 60611

Colorado Press Photographers Association
1711 South Newport Way
Denver, CO 80202

Connecticut News Photographers Association
180 Goodwin Street
Bristol, CT 06010

Cooperstate Press Photographers Association
Box 465
Tempe, AZ 85281

Dakotas Press Photographers Association
2929 8th Street
Fargo, ND 58102

Educational Film Library Association
43 West 61st Street
New York, NY 10023

Evidence Photographers International
601 Brookview Court
Oxford, OH 45056

Federal and International Media Communicators
Box 23620

L'Enfant Post Office
Washington, DC 20024

Graphic Arts Technical Foundation
4615 Forbes Avenue
Pittsburgh, PA 15213

Gravure Technical Association
60 East 42nd Street
New York, NY 10017

**Houston Gulf-Coast
News Photographers Association**
12411 Longbrook
Houston, TX 77072

Film and Video Communicators/ IFPA
3518 Cahuenga Boulevard West
Hollywood, CA 90068

Illinois Press Photographers Association
3345 West 91st Street
Evergreen Park, IL 60642

Indiana News Photographers Association
3930 Ivory Way
Indianapolis IN 46227

Industrial Photographers Association of New York
c/o Sanford Speiser
51 West 52nd Street
New York, NY 10019

**Industrial Photographers Association
of New Jersey**
232 Central Avenue
Caldwell, NJ 07006

Information Film Producers of America
Box 1470
Hollywood, CA 90028

**International Alliance of
Theatrical and Stage Employees (IATSE)**
Local 644
250 West 57th Street
New York, NY 10019

IATSE - Local 659
7715 Sunset Boulevard
Hollywood, CA 90046

IATSE - Local 666
327 South LaSalle Street
Chicago, IL 60604

International Fire Photographers Association
588 West De Koven Street
Chicago, IL 60647

International Photographers Association
2063 North Leavitt
Chicago, IL 60647

**International Photographers of
Motion Picture Industry**
Local 644
250 West 57th Street
New York, NY 10019

International Photo Optics Association
1156 Avenue of the Americas
New York, NY 10036

International Society for Photogrammetry
Piazza Leonardo Da Vinci, 32
Milan, Italy 20133

International Color Council
c/o Department of Chemistry
Rensselaer Polytechnic Inst.
Troy, NY 12181

Michigan Press Photographers Association
Box 1731
Grand Rapids, MI 49501

Milwaukee Press Photographers Association
35 East Van Norman Avenue
Cudahy, WI 53110

**National Association of
Government Communicators**
P.O. Box 1590
Arlington, VA 22210

**National Association of
Photographic Equipment Technicians**
1240 Mt. Olive Road
Washington, DC 20002

**National Association of
Photographic Manufacturers**
600 Mamaroneck Avenue
Harrison, NY 10528

National Audio-Visual Assn.
3150 Spring Street
Fairfax, VA 22030

National Directory of Camera Collectors
Box 4246
Santa Barbara, CA 93103

National Free Lance Photographers Association
Four East State Street
Doylestown, PA 18901

National Microfilm Association
8728 Colesville Road
Silver Spring, MD 20910

National Press Photographers Association
Box 1146
Durham, NC 27702

Nebraska Press Photographers Association
206 Avery Hall
University of Nebraska
Lincoln, NE 68508

New Jersey Press Photographers Association
91 Douglas Street
Lambertville, NJ 08530

New York Press Photographers Association
225 East 36th Street
New York, NY 10016

Ohio News Photographers Association
1446 Conneaut Avenue
Bowling Green, OH 43402

Oklahoma News Photographers Association
830 Crestview
Ada, OK 74820

Ophthalmic Photographers Society
Cabrini Health Care Center
227 East 19th Street
New York, NY 10003

Pennsylvania Press Photographers Association
1919 South Broad Street
Lansdale, PA 19446

Photo Chemical Machinery Institute
1717 Howard Street
Evanston, IL 60201

Photo Marketing Association
603 Lansing Avenue
Jackson, MI 49202

Photographic Administrators
Three Province Lane
Glen Head, NY 11545

Photographic Credit Institute
370 Lexington Avenue
New York, NY 10017

Photographic Historical Society of America
Box 1839
Radio City Station
New York, NY 10019

Photographic Manufacturers and Distributors Association
866 UN Plaza
New York, NY 10017

Photographic Society of America
2005 Walnut Street
Philadelphia, PA 19103

Press Photographers Assoc. of Long Island
Five Firelight Court
Dix Hills, NY 11746

Professional Photographers Guild of Florida
Box 1307
Homestead, FL 33030

Professional Photographers of America
1090 Executive Way
Des Plaines, IL 60618

Professional Photographers of Canada
318 Royal Bank Building
Edmonton, Alberta T5J 1W8
Canada

Professional Photographers of San Francisco
44 Montgomery Street
San Francisco, CA 94104

Puget Sound Press Photographers Association
16823 1st Street Southeast
Bothell, WA 98011

Royal Photographic Society
145 Audley Street
London, W1, England

Societe Francaise de Photographie et de Cinematographie
9 rue Montalembert
Paris, France VII

Society for Photographic Education
Box 1651
FDR Station
New York, NY 10022

Society of Motion Picture and Television Engineers
862 Scarsdale Avenue
Scarsdale, NY 10583

Society of Northern Ohio Professional Photographers
23611 Chagrin Boulevard
Beachwood, OH 44122

Society of Photo-Optical Instrumentation Engineers
Box 10
405 Fieldston Road
Bellingham, WA 98225

Society of Photographers and Artists Representatives
Box 845
FDR Station
New York, NY 10022

Society of Photographic Scientists and Engineers
1411 K Street N.W.
Washington, DC 20005

Society of Photo-Optical Instrumentation Engineers
338 Tejon Place
Palos Verdes Estates, CA 90274

Society of Photo-Technologists
Box 3174
Aurora, CO 80041

South Florida News Photographers Association
Box 3107
Miami, FL 33101

Studio Suppliers Association
548 Goffle Road
Hawthorne, NJ 07506

Underwater Photography Society
Box 15921
Los Angeles, CA 90015

United States Senate Press Photography Gallery
United States Senate
Room S-317
Washington, DC 20510

University Photographers Association of America
c/o Photographic Services Department
Austin Peay University
Clarksville, TN 37040

Wedding Photographers of America
Box 66218
Los Angeles, CA 90066

White House News Photographers Association
1515 L Street N.W.
Washington, DC 20005

VOLUNTEER LAWYERS FOR THE ARTS

Volunteer Lawyers for the Arts--the VLA--was founded in New York City in 1969 to provide artists and arts organizations with the legal assistance they needed but were not able to afford. Today, New York alone has approximately 900 lawyers volunteering their time and help, and most states have a VLA chapter and there is one in Toronto as well.

Each VLA chapter is different; some offer seminars, conferences, and news letters; others provide accounting and business advice; some have financial requirements for eligibility; and some charge minimal fees for services. Contact the VLA nearest you to find out more about it or, for a directory listing all the VLAs and all the services they provide, write to the New York City VLA, including $2 to cover postage ($1 for subsequent copies).

Bay Area Lawyers for the Arts (BALA)
Fort Mason Center, Bldg. C
San Francisco, CA 94123

Los Angeles VLA
P.O. Box 57008
Los Angeles, CA 90057

San Diego Lawyers for the Arts
1295 Prospect St., Suite C
La Jolla, CA 92037

Canadian Artists Representation Ontario (CARO)
345-67 Mowat Avenue
Toronto, Ontario M6K 3E3
Canada

Colorado Lawyers for the Arts (COLA)
770 Pennsylvania
Denver, CO 80203

Connecticut Volunteer Lawyers for the Arts (CTVLA)
Connecticut Commission on the Arts
190 Trumbull Street
Hartford, CT 06103-2206

D.C. Lawyers Committee for the Arts (LCA)
Volunteer Lawyers for the Arts
918 16th St., N.W., Suite 503
Washington, DC 20006

D.C. Washington Area Lawyers for the Arts (WALA)
2025 I St. N.W., Suite 608
Washington, DC 20006

Volunteer Lawyers for the Arts Program
Pinellas County Arts Council
400 Pierce Boulevard
Clearwater, FL 33516

Broward Arts Council
  100 S. Andrews Avenue
  Fort Lauderdale, FL 33301

Business Volunteers for the Arts/Miami
  c/o Greater Miami Chamber of Commerce
  1601 Biscayne Boulevard
  Miami, FL 33132

**Liaison to the Entertainment and
Arts Law Committee**
  Public Interest Programs
  Florida Bar Association
  600 Appalachee Parkway
  Tallahassee, FL 32301-8226

Georgia Volunteer Lawyers for the Arts (GVLA)
  32 Peachtree St., Suite 521
  Atlanta, GA 30303

Lawyers for the Creative Arts (LCA)
  623 S. Wabash Avenue Suite 300-N
  Chicago, IL 60605

Volunteer Lawyers for the Arts Committee
  Cedar Rapids/Marion Arts Council
  424 First Avenue, N.E.
  Cedar Rapids, IA 52407

Barry Lindahl
  622 Dubuque Building
  Dubuque, IA 52201

Dee Peretz
  Lexington Council of the Arts
  161 N. Mill Street
  Lexington, KY 40507

Community Arts Council
  609 W. Main St.
  Louisville, KY 40202

Louisiana Volunteer Lawyers for the Arts (LVLA)
  c/o Arts Council of New Orleans
  ITM Bldg., Suite 936
  Two Canal Street
  New Orleans, LA 70130

Maine Volunteer Lawyers for the Arts Project
  Maine State Commission
    on the Arts & the Humanities
  55 Capitol Street
  State House Station 25
  Augusta, ME 04333

Maryland Lawyers for the Arts
  c/o University of Baltimore Law School
  1420 N. Charles Street
  Baltimore, MD 21201

The Arts Extension Service (AES)
  Div. of Continuing Education
  University of Massachusetts
  Amherst, MA 01003

Lawyers & Accountants for the Arts
  The Artists Foundation
  110 Broad Street
  Boston, MA 02169

Michigan Volunteer Lawyers for the Arts (MVLA)
  1283 Leeward Drive
  Okemos, MI 48864

Minnesota Volunteer Lawyers for the Arts (MVLA)
  c/o Fred Rosenblatt
  100 S. 5th St., Suite 1500
  Minneapolis, MN 55402

**St. Louis Volunteer Lawyers & Accountants
for the Arts (SLVLAA)**
  c/o St. Louis Regional, Cultural &
    Performing Arts Development Commission
  329 N. Euclid Avenue
  St. Louis, MO 63108

Montana Volunteer Lawyers for the Arts
  c/o Joan Jonkel
  P.O. Box 8687
  Missoula, MT 69807

Volunteer Lawyers for the Arts of New Jersey
  A special project of the
    Center for Non-Profit Corporations
  36 W. Lafayette Street
  Trenton, NJ 08608

Volunteer Lawyers for the Arts Program
  Albany League of Arts
  19 Clinton Avenue
  Albany, NY 12207

Arts Council in Buffalo & Erie County
  700 Main Street
  Buffalo, NY 14202

Huntington Arts Council
  213 Main Street
  Huntington, NY 11743

Volunteer Lawyers for the Arts (VLA)
1560 Broadway, Suite 711
New York, NY 10036

Dutchess County Arts Council (DCAC)
12 Vassar Street
Poughkeepsie, NY 12601

**North Carolina Volunteer Lawyers
for the Arts (NCVLA)**
P.O. Box 590
Raleigh, NC 27602

**Cincinnati Area Lawyers & Accountants
for the Arts**
ML003
University of Cincinnati
Cincinnati, OH 45221

Volunteer Lawyers for the Arts Program
c/o Cleveland Bar Assoc.
Mall Building
118 St. Clair Avenue
Cleveland, OH 44114

Arnold Gottlieb
421 N. Michigan Street
Toledo, OH 43624

Betty Price
State Arts Council of Oklahoma
Room 640
Jim Thorpe Building
Oklahoma City, OK 73105-4987

**Philadelphia Volunteer Lawyers
for the Arts (PVLA)**
251 S. 18th Street
Philadelphia, PA 19103

Ocean State Lawyers for the Arts (OSLA)
96 Sachem Road
Narragansett, RI 02882

South Carolina Lawyers for the Arts (SCLA)
P.O. Box 10023
Greenville, NC 29603

Bennett Tarleton
Tennessee Arts Commission
320 Sixth Avenue North
Nashville, TN 37219

**Austin Lawyers & Accountants
for the Arts (ALAA)**
P.O. Box 2577
Austin, TX 78768

**Volunteer Lawyers & Accountants
for the Arts (VLAA)**
1540 Sul Ross
Houston, TX 77006

Utah Lawyers for the Arts (ULA)
50 S. Main, Suite 900
Salt Lake City, UT 84144

Washington Lawyers for the Arts (WVLA)
428 Joseph Vance Building
1402 Third Avenue
Seattle, WA 98101